GENNADY AYGI

Selected Poems 1954–94

GENNADY AYGI was born in 1934 in the village of Shaymurzino, in the Chuvash Autonomous Republic, some 500 miles east of Moscow; his father was a village schoolteacher, his maternal grandfather a priest of the ancient Chuvash religion. Although he writes mainly in Russian, Aygi is regarded as the Chuvash national poet; he has translated poetry of many languages into Chuvash and has edited a historic anthology of Chuvash poetry.

Expelled from the Gorky Literary Institute and the Komsomol because of his links with Pasternak, Aygi found a society of like-minded artists in the creative Moscow underground. For ten years he worked at the Mayakovsky Museum, organizing exhibitions of modern art, but generally he led a life of poverty, constantly harassed by officialdom, and earning a living principally by translation into Chuvash. His many "books" of poetry remained unpublished in the Soviet Union until the end of the 1980s, but at the same time his work was published and acclaimed throughout the world, being translated into some twenty (including most European) languages. He lives with his wife in Moscow and has six children.

PETER FRANCE was born in Londonderry in 1935. After reading French and Russian at Oxford, he taught first at the University of Sussex and from 1980 at the University of Edinburgh, where he was Professor of French, 1980–90 and is now an Endowment Fellow. His books on French and Russian literature include the *New Oxford Companion to Literature in French* (1995) and *Poets of Modern Russia* (Cambridge University Press, 1982). He has translated Blok, Pasternak and Brodsky, two previous short volumes of poetry by Aygi, and Aygi's *Anthology of Chuvash Poetry* (Forest Books, 1991). His translations of Aygi's work have benefited from his close friendship with the poet over a number of years.

GENNADY AYGI

Selected Poems
1954–94

Edited with translations by
PETER FRANCE

Bilingual edition

ANGEL BOOKS
London

First published by
Angel Books, 3 Kelross Road, London N5 2QS
1 3 5 7 9 10 8 6 4 2

British Library Cataloguing in Publication data:
A catalogue record for this book is available from the British Library

ISBN 0 946162 59 X

This book is printed on Permanent Paper conforming to the
recommendations of the British Library

Funded by
THE
ARTS
COUNCIL
OF ENGLAND

Typeset in Great Britain by
The Ukrainian Information Service Ltd, London

Printed and bound by
Woolnough Bookbinding Ltd, Irthlingborough, Northamptonshire

"And until then – ever further – into the snows. Into naked poverty. How few things were needed. Hands – only a little more. A poem... – all so little, all more and more – without us – the World."

Gennady Aygi, *Poetry-as-Silence*, 1992

Содержание

Contents

Acknowledgements

Acknowledgement is due to the publishers of the following journals and books, in which earlier versions of some of these translations first appeared:

Adam
Cencrastus
Chapman
Comparative Criticism
Essays in Poetics
Frank
Gnosis
Index on Censorship
Lines Review
Modern Poetry in Translation
South-East Arts Review
Tel Aviv Review
Temenos
Times Literary Supplement
Verse

G. Aygi, *Veronica's Book*, tr. P. France, Polygon, Edinburgh, 1989
G. Aygi, *Salute – to Singing*, tr. P. France, Akros, Edinburgh, 1995
P. France, *Poets of Modern Russia*, Cambridge University Press, 1982
J. Glad and D. Weissbort (eds), *Russian Poetry, the Modern Period*, 2nd ed., University of Iowa Press, Iowa City, IA, 1993
J. Kates (ed.), *In the Grip of Strange Thoughts: Russian Poetry in a New Era*, Zephyr Press, Somerville, MA, 1997
P. Mortimer and S. J. Litherland (eds), *The Poetry of Perestroika*, Iron Press, North Shields, 1991

Aygi's preferred text of his poems has been followed throughout this volume. The translations were made direct from the poet's typescripts, but have been checked against the following publications, which in some cases contain amended versions:

G. Aygi, *Otmechennaya zima*, ed. V. Losskaya, Syntaxis, Paris, 1982

G. Aïgui, *Le Cahier de Véronique*, bilingual edition with French translation by L. Robel, Le Nouveau Commerce, Paris, 1984

Le Nouveau Commerce, cahier 67, Spring 1987

G. Aïgui, *Le Temps des Ravines*, bilingual edition with French translation by L. Robel, Le Nouveau Commerce, Paris, 1990

G. Aygi, *Zdes'*, Sovremennik, Moscow, 1991

G. Aygi, *Teper' vsegda snega*, Sovetskiy Pisatel', Moscow, 1992

G. Ajgi, *Gruss dem Gesang*, bilingual edition with German translation by F. P. Ingold, Rainer Verlag, Berlin, 1992

G. Ajgi, *Die letzte Fahrt*, bilingual edition with German translation by F. P. Ingold, Rainer Verlag, Berlin, 1993

Segodnya, Moscow, 14 January 1995

G. Aygi, *Strana-Prolog*, Izdaniye N. Dronnikova, Paris, 1995

I should like to express my gratitude to the publishers of all of these.

Introduction

"Let me be in your midst / a dusty coin turning up / among rustling banknotes / in a slippery silk purse" – with these words, the opening lines of the first poem in the present selection, the twenty-year-old Chuvash poet Gennady Aygi proclaimed his otherness, his wish to hold on to difference in a time of conformity. The stance is youthfully Romantic, reminiscent of one of Aygi's first poetic models, that great outsider Vladimir Mayakovsky. Mayakovsky maintained his spectacular isolation until his final suicide; he was his own tragic hero. Aygi, by contrast, speaks less and less of himself, dissolving his individuality in the life of the world and other people, yet he has continued to speak with an utterly original voice.

For many Russian readers, he has the reputation of a difficult, hermetic poet. It is therefore worth insisting at the outset that his poems are concerned with common human experience, with fundamental values, questions and aspirations. They are not just poems for a highly sophisticated élite. A group of Chuvash teenagers, confronted with his poetry by their teacher, recognized their difficulty, but responded with enthusiasm and understanding. Here are just two of their comments: "Aygi's poems go deep into my soul. They strike me by the depth of their thought, you have to think about them a lot, penetrate into their meaning"; "Aygi's writings help us to understand this complicated world, they force us to think about things we never thought about, they teach us to believe. Aygi becomes more and more intelligible to us."[1]

In attempting to place his poetry, one could do worse than to situate it at the opposite pole from that of Joseph Brodsky. Brodsky took his place with regal ease as the heir to those we have come to see as the great names of twentieth-century Russian poetry: Blok, Akhmatova, Pasternak, Mandelshtam, Tsvetayeva. Growing up in the Petersburg of Pushkin and Akhmatova, he seemed at home – even in exile and distress – in a powerful cultural tradition that finds expression in the rich sounds and semantic complexities of high formal verse.

Aygi does not belong here. Russian is not his first language; he was born (in 1934) in the Chuvash Autonomous Republic, where he grew up in the countryside, 500 miles from Moscow and Petersburg.[2] Until he discovered Mayakovsky in 1948, he knew virtually no modern Russian poetry. Later he became very attached to such Russian poets as Lermontov and Annensky, and one might also see in his poems echoes of the Symbolists, but he himself, particularly early on, stressed his indebtedness to the mould-breaking Russian modernism whose principal poetic voices are two provincials, Mayakovsky from the Caucasus and the great and inaccessible Velimir Khlebnikov from Astrakhan, together with such radical futurists as Aleksey Kruchonykh and the experimental poets of 1920s Leningrad, Daniil Kharms, Aleksandr Vvedensky and Nikolay Zabolotsky. Equally important for him – perhaps more so – was that other barbarian of genius, the painter Kazimir Malevich;[3] organizing exhibitions in the Mayakovsky Museum in Moscow from 1959 to 1969, he amassed a remarkable knowledge of the arts of the Russian avant-garde of the early twentieth century.

Outsider though he may be, Aygi has made or discovered his own spiritual and artistic family, going beyond Russia to embrace writers and thinkers of Europe and Asia. At the Gorky Literary Institute in Moscow, where he studied from 1953 to 1959, he read assiduously, and taught himself French. Thus he discovered Baudelaire, the essential poet, and after him the whole range of modern French poetry, culminating in René Char, to whom he has written a moving tribute.[4] In 1968 he published an extraordinary anthology of French poetry, ranging from Villon to Bonnefoy, translated into his native Chuvash; this sold out immediately in Chuvashia and won him a prize from the Académie Française. Equally important have been such masters of European modernism as Kierkegaard, Nietzsche and Kafka, together with a whole galaxy of religious thinkers from many different countries. Spiritually the "Chuvash boy" (to quote Yevtushenko's introduction to the first Russian edition of Aygi's poems) is a citizen of the world.

This cosmopolitan openness, allied with the rebellious originality of his poetry, quickly set him at odds with the Soviet authorities. The tension was exacerbated in the late 1950s by his friendship with Boris Pasternak. At a time when the Nobel Prize affair was raging after the publication of *Doctor Zhivago* in

1957,[5] Aygi was Pasternak's neighbour in the writers' village of Peredelkino, where the older poet befriended and encouraged the young student. In 1959 Aygi was expelled from both the Komsomol and the Literary Institute as an alien element. As he put it in an interview published in *Index on Censorship* in 1993:

> ... after 1958, because of the case against Pasternak, I was excluded from literary circles. I could not return to Chuvashia, my life would have been threatened, so I remained in Moscow without a permit or money, and spent the nights on railway stations. But in 1959 I was lucky enough to meet a group of underground artists, writers and musicians. It saved me. We shared the same passionate concerns and interests.

And so he became a writer of the "underground". This was to be his support system at a time of great material hardship. Though a victim of the régime, he was not generally active in political dissident movements, but in the company of kindred spirits such as the composer Andrey Volkonsky or the painters Vladimir Yakovlev and Igor Vulokh, he pursued a lonely poetic task, scraping a living with translations into Chuvash, but writing book after book of poetry. All of this remained unpublished in the Soviet Union. But from the early 1960s – first in Eastern Europe, then in France, Germany and elsewhere – he was being published both in translation and in Russian, and gradually acquired his current European reputation as one of the most important Russian-language poets of our time.

Such foreign fame did not endear him to the Writers' Union in the Soviet Union, particularly when his poems were published in the émigré journal *Kontinent* in 1975. It was only with *glasnost'* that the first halting steps were taken to publish his Russian poems in Russia and Chuvashia – the first swallow being a fifteen-page pamphlet published as a supplement to the Chuvash newspaper *Young Communist* in 1987. Since then large selections of his work have been published in Moscow, the first with a preface by the representative of the semi-official poetry of his generation, Yevgeny Yevtushenko. Though his poems fly in the face of many Russian habits and expectations, he has now gained something of the status of a modern classic, the most important representative of the contemporary Russian poetic avant-garde.

If European modernism is one side to Aygi's writing, the other vital element is his native Chuvash culture. The Chuvash people, close on two million in number, are descended from the ancient Huns and Bulgars. Most of them live in a territory about the size of Wales, on the great bend of the Volga between Nizhny Novgorod (previously Gorky) and Kazan. Since the mid-sixteenth century, Chuvashia has been administratively a part of Russia, and over the centuries the Chuvash were subjected to forced Russification and Christianization. Nevertheless, in their own "underground", taking refuge in their ravines and forests, they have retained their Turkic language – a language utterly different from Russian. The ancient pagan religion has largely disappeared, but many elements of the traditional rural culture – not least a poetic culture in a land where "every tenth peasant is a poet" – survive side by side with the results of Soviet urbanization and industrialization.

Aygi was born in August 1934 in the village of Shaymurzino, in the depths of the southern Chuvash countryside. When I first visited Shaymurzino in 1989 (until then the whole region was out of bounds to foreigners), it was still, in spite of modern machinery, schools and so on, a place in which you could feel the old way of life, set among the great fields of black earth, the forests and ravines which figure so prominently in Aygi's poetry. The hospitable village of wooden houses and stockyards, with its muddy streets full of children and geese, is flanked by an old cemetery, full of bent wooden crosses, where we poured libations of beer and honey on the tomb of Aygi's maternal grandfather, one of the last pagan "priests" of the village.

His father, Nikolay Lisin (Aygi is an adopted name, a tribal name meaning "that one himself"), was a village teacher of Russian; he was killed at the front in 1942. Apart from a brief spell in Karelia (now in Finland) Gennady attended village schools in Chuvashia and from 1949 to 1953 a local teachers' training college. Then, having attracted the attention and affection of one of the leading Chuvash poets, Peder Khuzangay, he was able in 1953 to go and study at the Literary Institute in Moscow, and since then the capital has been his main home. He has married four times and has six children, five boys and one girl (Veronika).

In the late 1950s, encouraged by Pasternak and others, Aygi went over to writing poetry directly in Russian (before then he had translated his own Chuvash verse). The choice of Russian gave him access to international literary culture, making it easier for him to communicate with readers throughout the world.

It also inevitably meant distancing himself from his Chuvash roots; indeed he has said that in his youth he avoided Chuvash folklore because its forms seemed primitive to one whose masters were the great modernists. Yet the vital connection remained, embodied perhaps most fully in the figure of his mother, whose death is the subject of one of his earliest poems to be written directly in Russian, "Death". In the decades since 1960, and particularly since about 1980, he has grown ever more attached to his ancestral culture, recognizing and celebrating its continuing value in modern times. This attachment has shown itself firstly in his production of volumes of French, Polish and Hungarian poetry in Chuvash translation; these have enriched the poetic possibilities open to his compatriots. Secondly, over a period of ten years, he put together a remarkable anthology of Chuvash folklore and poetry which has been translated into a number of European languages.[6] By 1994, the year of his sixtieth birthday, the poet who had once been harassed or cold-shouldered as a cosmopolitan decadent was being celebrated as the Chuvash national poet.

What does Aygi the poet owe to Chuvash culture? Not so much its poetic forms (he has always eschewed the pastiche of folklore) as a whole world of images – trees, fields, clearings, ravines – and above all a set of values which he describes in his introduction to the Chuvash anthology: a veneration for old people, including the weak and helpless; a sense of family and community; a bond between humanity and the natural world ("a Chuvash knows that the river is a god, that the forest speaks, that it too is a god, and that our fathers are embodied in the trees"). It is primarily from Chuvash culture, I think, that he derives the fusion of the aesthetic, the ethical and the spiritual which grounds his own poetic work.

To Gennady Aygi's distinctive fusion of European and Russian modernism with the ancient Chuvash tradition not all Russians are sympathetic: many see his free verse as both too hermetic and too neglectful of the normal patterns of Russian verse. A Western reader too may find it difficult at first – though probably not more so than much contemporary poetry from continental Europe – but I think the Chuvash teenagers were right to say that as one reads one's way into it, letting poems answer one another and work in the mind, much that had seemed obscure is decanted into the bright clarity of which Aygi so often writes.[7]

The poems of the 1960s and 1970s in particular are permeated with the notion of sleep. A set of notes called "Sleep-and-Poetry", written in 1975, speaks of the rich reservoirs available to the sleeping person:

> And even so, "let us plunge into the night" (Kafka).
> There are people there. There, in the depths of sleep, is the communion of the living and the dead.
> And just as we do not picture the souls of the dead as "social" or "national", so, if only in sleep, let us be trustful in the souls of the living, – and for this let us wish ourselves clear sleep, *sleep* which seems to have forgotten us.
> For who besides Poetry would allow himself to do this? ...[8]

For Aygi the creative experience is closer to sleep or dream than to rational wakefulness, and poetry is very different from purposeful, persuasive speech. It is more akin to the rustle of grasses, of trees, of flowers (see "Rustle of birches"), at the limits of intelligibility. Or again, it is like the as yet unformed speech of the infant; in the introduction to *Veronica's Book*, which is devoted to the "wordless" yet "creative" early months of his daughter, he writes of the similarity between her childish "babble" and the state of the poet before writing, "this quietness which 'contains something', this kind of 'buzz', the still unformed intonation and the special searching power; the gaps in the rhythm and the tense pauses fuller of meaning than any particular 'sense'".[9]

For Aygi then, the creative impulse is only partly conscious; it is at odds with the heroic wakefulness of the orator or the political poet. Yet he is in no sense a naïve writer; he works over his poems meticulously and is keenly aware of what he is doing. Over the years, though he has been reluctant to explain particular poems, he has given many interviews explaining his poetic aims and practice. His craftsmanlike approach to work with words may be compared to that of Mayakovsky, even if the Futurist's loud public poetry is at the opposite pole from his quiet work.

A lot of this work is devoted to syntax. As he put it in an early interview, in order to express insights that resist normal utterance and to find a way of writing adequate to the human situation in the modern world, he dislocates the normal ordering of words, trying to "reconstruct it in accordance with the changes that in my opinion have taken place in the language of relationships between people". Lacking many of the articulations of ordinary prose, with its clear transitions and distinctions, Aygi's poems are nevertheless carefully constructed down to the smallest detail. Habitual punctuation is replaced by his own system, in which capitals, italics, spaced letters, brackets, colons, dashes and suspension points are deployed in a highly original way.[10] Although his vocabulary range is deliberately limited, he will sometimes create new words; in particular he uses hyphens to create composite words of the kind more common in languages less analytic than the Indo-European. The spatial organization of words on the page and the surrounding whiteness are essential too – sometimes one is reminded of Malevich writing about Suprematist art: "these masses will hang in space and enable our consciousness to penetrate ever further from the earth".[11]

This is free verse of course, with only occasional ventures into traditional prosody. The sound of words is crucial (and obviously very difficult for the translator) – not only the values of consonants and vowels, but the rhythmical patterns formed by words. Line lengths can vary dramatically, but surprisingly often the dislocations and discontinuities apparent in the poem as visual object are overridden by a powerful, frequently ternary, rhythm, which recalls the incantations of the Chuvash pagan religion. When Aygi reads his poems aloud, these sonorities are given full play in his deliberate delivery.

The poems form two main groups. One of these consists of occasional pieces, arranged in two open-ended collections, *Winter Revels* and *Poems of Various Years*. Aygi's principal work, however, is a series of "books" which together can be seen as a single extended volume. Within the overall series each book forms a unity in which themes, images and words echo one another. As things have turned out, however, it has rarely been possible to publish the books separately, with the exception of the much translated *Veronica's Book*.

In the present selection, one book only is presented complete, *Quietness-Premonition*. This is made up of poems written in 1974–76, before and after the death of Aygi's close friend the poet and translator Konstantin Bogatyryov, a free spirit who having been condemned to death and then sent to a labour camp under Stalin, was murdered in 1976 outside his Moscow flat, in all probability by agents of the KGB. In *Quietness-Pre-*

monition Aygi brings together quiet, sometimes ecstatic poems
written one or two years before Bogatyryov's death with poems
where the rawness of the poet's grief struggles to find some
consolation. In retrospect, therefore, the exalted vulnerability
of the earlier poems takes on a special poignancy, as if the
hushed silence already contained the violence whose eruption is
ominously sensed in "Note: Apophatic". Four of the poems take
up in their titles the word *tishina* (quietness), but there are many
other echoes of word or image from poem to poem – most of
all, in this book, that of gold. In "Willow branch at the window"
the sun at the window is golden, and so is the soul, emblemat-
ized in the willow branch, but gold figures also in several of the
earlier poems, most strikingly perhaps in "Forest places: variation" which can be seen as prefiguring the later poem – though
in a more positive vein – in the assertion of solidarity and spir-
ituality against the brutality of the régime.

Reading all the poems of a given book in relation to one
another heightens the resonance of local images, then, but between books too, and across the years, there are powerful net-
works of association. Over a period of forty years there has nat-
urally been change and development in both the form and the
dominant concerns of Aygi's writing. Recently, for instance, the
Chuvash element has come more to the fore, particularly in
Salute – to Singing, one of his most accessible pieces. Nevertheless, the dominant impression left by his work is one of
remarkable continuity from the 1950s to the present. His
poems have their source in vital questions about our being in
the world, and they explore this is a manner which is all his
own, using a poetic language of which the essential features
were already in place by 1960.

Compared with the work of a poet whom in some other
respects he resembles, Gerard Manley Hopkins, Aygi's poetry
could be described as "poor" poetry, pared down to the essential. It is indeed this poverty, linked as it is with such positive
themes as whiteness, light, pain, ecstasy and divine presence,
that gives his writing its special quality, like Malevich's "white on
white". His poems may offer striking images, but they contain
little of the rich evocation of physical reality that one finds in a
Mandelshtam or a Brodsky; much is general, imprecise or tentative. Even so, they are usually located in a specific setting, and
start from a particular object or moment, often indicated in the
title. Frequently the starting-point is in the natural world of

trees and flowers, fields, forests and rivers, that world that is so closely bound to humanity in traditional Chuvash culture. In the "rose poems" of 1966 for instance, the vulnerable white flowers are an analogue for human desire and fragility:

> and into faces
> destroying comes
> damp fracturation
> of whiteness

In a sense, Aygi is no doubt a "nature poet", but his work is concerned with fundamental spiritual realities, the absence or the presence of a transcendental element in the world. In this way it engages with the basic needs of human beings, emphasizing the kinship between them. "Poetry", he once wrote, "is always for me that kind of 'action' and 'connection' which is best expressed by the words 'religious rite'".[12] So the theme of human friendship runs through poems that may at first seem like the meditations of a solitary. They are often dedicated or addressed to particular friends, but Aygi reaches out beyond this circle. One of his occasional poems is simply a blank sheet of paper into which the reader is invited to fold a flower picked during a walk.

Especially in the connection between people which it embodies, Aygi's work can be read as a response to the political and social conditions of the time, most of it belonging to the Brezhnev era. It is a deeply tragic poetry, a response to the tragic twentieth century of global war, genocide and the anguished loss of old beliefs. Political questions are hardly ever openly addressed here, but there is a constant sense of solidarity with the victims of hardship and physical violence. Words such as "poor", "beggarly", "cut" or "beat" recur, and are associated with positive images of light, whiteness or fire. Such is the case with "Willow branch at the window" (in *Quietness-Premonition*) and with the remarkable meditative sequence of 1988, *Final Departure*, devoted to the heroic life and tragic fate of Raoul Wallenberg and through him to the victims of the Holocaust.

One of Aygi's central books, *Time of Gratitude*, written in 1976–77, carries an epigraph attributed to Plato: "Night is the best time for believing in the light." Light, with quietness and sleep, is a major leitmotif of his writing. He works to bring hope out of despair, finding support in the natural world, art and religion, traditional Chuvash values, and the restorative power of sleep. Of all his works, the most positive is *Veronica's Book*, devoted to the first six months of his daughter's life. Here he tries to find words both for his feelings as a father and for the wordless experience of the child. It is no accident that in doing so he returns repeatedly to his own childhood and his Chuvash origins.

The texts and translations that follow offer a selection from forty years of poetry. I have tried to choose poems that give a representative view of Aygi's work at different periods. This has meant that with the exception of *Quietness-Premonition* no book could be included in full. For complete translations of other single books, the reader could look at my versions of *Veronica's Book* and *Salute – to Singing*.[13]

In translating, I have remained close to the letter of the original and have tried to resist the strong temptation to normalize or domesticate Aygi's distinctive writing. If the result is sometimes disconcerting, I hope that readers will find this an ultimately positive experience, as I have. I began translating Aygi in order to gain a better understanding of poetry that tantalized me with the promise of a significance which at first eluded me. Even so, there is much that remains tentative, and much more that defeats my attempts to recreate it adequately in English. Those who are interested in the problems of translation might wish to look at my short essay on the translating of one poem ("Burning – during harvest").[14]

In working on these and other texts by Aygi over the past twenty years I have been helped by many people, including his translators into other languages, notably Léon Robel. It was Robin Milner-Gulland who first mentioned the name of Aygi to me in about 1973; since then I have received help and encouragement from a number of friends and colleagues: Troels Andersen, Galina Aygi, Robert Crawford, Julie Curtis, Nikolay Dronnikov, James Vladimir Gill, Duncan Glen, Michael Hamburger, Joy Hendry, Gerald Janecek, Atner Khuzangay, Angela Livingstone, Murdo MacDonald, Edwin Morgan, Valentina Polukhina, Jonathan Price, Kathleen Raine, Tessa Ransford, Paul Volsik, and many more. When it came to producing this volume, Rose France did valuable work preparing the Russian text for printing. Antony Wood of Angel Books has organized publication with great flair and enthusiasm, and I am most grateful for his support and his faith in the enterprise.

My principal debt, too great to repay, is to Gennady Aygi him-self. Not only has he helped me to a fuller understanding of his poetry, but since our first meeting in 1974 he has been a close friend, often distant in space, always present in mind. To trans-late his work has been to continue a conversation that was some-times interrupted for several years. This volume is my tribute to that friendship.

Peter France
Edinburgh, October 1996

NOTES

1 Quotations translated from *Vospriyatiye slova Aygi chitatelem* by G. A. Yermakova, Chuvash Educational Institute, Cheboksary, 1996.
2 There is very little material available in English about Chuvashia: see J. R. Krueger, *Chuvash Manual*, Bloomington, IN and The Hague, 1961, and G. Aygi, *An Anthology of Chuvash Poetry*, tr. P. France, London, 1991.
3 On Aygi and Malevich, see G. Aygi, "Kasimir Malevich and other poems", tr. with an introduction by Peter France, *Comparative Criticism*, 4 (1982), pp. 269-80.
4 "Sur la mort de René Char", in G. Aïgui, *Conversations à distance*, tr. L. Robel, Saulxures, France, 1994, pp. 195-98.
5 The publication of *Doctor Zhivago* in Italian translation in November 1957 gave rise to a bitter campaign against Pasternak in the Soviet Union; he was expelled from the Writers' Union and pressured into refusing the Nobel Prize for Literature in 1958.
6 The first version to appear was in Italian; for details of the English trans-lation, a shortened version, see note 2 above.
7 For a reading of three Aygi poems see Appendix: "Reading Aygi".
8 G. Aygi, *Veronica's Book, with Notes on Sleep-and-Poetry*, tr. P. France, Edinburgh, 1989, p. 101.
9 *Veronica's Book*, p. 13.
10 On Aygi's punctuation, see G. Janecek, "The Poetics of Punctuation in Gennadyj Ajgi's Verse", *Slavic and East European Journal*, 40, 2 (1996).
11 K. S. Malevich, *Essays on Art, 1915–1933*, ed. T. Andersen, tr. X. Glowacki-Prus and A. McMillin, London, 1969, I, 51.
12 From notes on his poetry published in G. Ajgi, *Stichi, 1954–1971*, ed. W. Kasack, Munich, 1975, p. 195.
13 See Further Reading.
14 P. France, "Translating a Chuvash Poet: Gennady Aygi", *Comparative Criticism*, 16 (1994), pp. 187-94.

Selected Poems
1954–94

ЗАВЯЗЬ

пускай я буду среди вас
как пыльная монета оказавшаяся
среди шуршащих ассигнаций
в шелковом скользком кармане:
звенеть бы ей во весь голос
да не с чем сталкиваться чтобы звенеть

когда гудят контрабасы
и когда вспоминается
как в детстве ветер
дымил дождем в осеннее утро –

пускай я буду
стоячей вешалкой
на которую можно
вешать не только плащи
но можно повесить еще что-нибудь
потяжелее плаща

и когда перестану я верить в себя
пусть память жил
вернет мне упорство
чтобы снова я стал на лице ощущать
давление мускулов глаз

1954

BEGINNING

let me be in your midst
a dusty coin turning up
among rustling banknotes
in a slippery silk purse:
it would ring at the top of its voice
but there's nothing hard to ring on

when double basses boom
and memory tells
how in childhood the wind
smoked with rain on autumn mornings

let me be
a standing coat-rack
on which you can hang
not raincoats only
but something besides
that weighs more than a coat

and when I stop believing in myself
let memory of veins
make me firm again
and again I shall feel
the eye muscles' pressure

1954

ПРЕДЧУВСТВИЕ РЕКВИЕМА

а вам отдохнуть не придется
и в ясном присутствии гроба его

вам предоставлена будет прохлада
как на открытой поляне
чернеющей и угасающей
как в окружении
деревьев черненных бесшумной корой

и явственней станет чем ваше "мы есть"
образа ясного свет
от которого будут болеть
ваши глаза с проявлением дна
с узкой – надглазной – костью
похожей на тусклый намордник

и станет известно что даже в то время
когда был горяч он насквозь
когда как ребенок был мягок и влажен
когда он хотел на прощанье сказать
три слова последние веры –

и приник ради этого
лицом небывало-доверчивым
к чему-то человеческому –

это и тогда оказалось
вашими руками

и запомним лицо остывающее
и все больше принимающее вид
маски вылепленной будто
руками убийц

1957

PRESENTIMENT OF A REQUIEM

but you will not even find rest
in his coffin's clear presence

to you will be offered a coolness
as in a woodland clearing
darkening and fading
as in a circle
of trees blackened by quiet bark

and more distinct than your "we are"
will be the clear image's light
that will make your eyeballs ache
laying bare the depths beneath
with narrow bone over eye
like a lustreless muzzle

and it shall be known that even
when he was shot through with warmth
soft and moist as a child
when he wanted to say farewell
in three last words of belief

and therefore bent low
a face unbelievably trusting
to something human

even then
he encountered your hands

and we shall remember the face as it sets
and more and more appears
a mask that seems moulded
by murderers' hands

1957

ЗДЕСЬ

словно чащи в лесу облюбована нами
суть тайников
берегущих людей

и жизнь уходила в себя как дорога в леса
и стало казаться ее иероглифом
мне слово "здесь"

и оно означает и землю и небо
и то что в тени
и то что мы видим воочью
и то чем делиться в стихах не могу

и разгадка бессмертия
не выше разгадки
куста освещенного зимнею ночью –

белых веток над снегом
черных теней на снегу

здесь все отвечает друг другу
языком первозданно-высоким
как отвечает – всегда высоко-необязанно –
жизни сверх-числовая свободная часть
смежной неуничтожаемой части

здесь
на концах ветром сломанных веток
притихшего сада
не ищем мы сгустков уродливых сока
на скорбные фигуры похожих –

обнимающих распятого
в вечер несчастья

и не знаем мы слова и знака
которые были бы выше другого
здесь мы живем и прекрасны мы здесь

HERE

like thickets in woodlands we have preferred
the essence of sanctuaries
sheltering people

and life led into itself like a road into woodlands
and I began to perceive as its hieroglyph
the one word "here"

and it means both earth and heaven
and what is in shadow
and what we can see face to face
and what I cannot share in my poems

and the riddle of immortality
is no harder to solve
than the riddle of bushes lit by winter nights

of white branches over the snow
of black shadows on the snow

here all things answer each other
in a high original tongue
as the unnumbered free part of life
– always lofty-unconstrained – gives answer
to the next indestructible part

here
on the tips of wind-broken branches
in the hushed garden
we do not seek ugly clots of sap
like grieving human figures –

kissing the crucified man
on the evening of disaster

and we know no word or sign
which is higher than the next
here we live and we are beautiful here

и здесь умолкая смущаем мы явь
но если прощание с нею сурово
то и в этом участвует жизнь –

как от себя же самой
нам неслышная весть

и от нас отодвинувшись
словно в воде отраженье куста
останется рядом она чтоб занять после нас
нам отслужившие
наши места –

чтобы пространства людей заменялись
только пространствами жизни
во все времена

1958

and here falling silent we shame the real
but if parting with it is harsh
yet life takes a part in this too

like an imperceptible
greeting from itself

and moving aside from us
like a bush reflected in water
it will wait on one side to take
our no longer needed
empty places

so that spaces of people should be followed
only by spaces of life
to the end of time

1958

СНЕГ

От близкого снега
цветы на подоконнике странны.

Ты улыбнись мне хотя бы за то,
что не говорю я слова,
которые никогда не пойму.
Все, что тебе я могу говорить:

стул, снег, ресницы, лампа.

И руки мои
просты и далеки,

и оконные рамы
будто вырезаны из белой бумаги,

а там, за ними,
около фонарей,
кружится снег

с самого нашего детства.

И будет кружиться, пока на земле
тебя вспоминают и с тобой говорят.

И эти белые хлопья когда-то
увидел я наяву,
и закрыл глаза, и не могу их открыть,
и кружатся белые искры,

и остановить их
я не могу.

1959–60

SNOW

From the nearby snow
the flowers on the sill are strange.

Smile to me if only because
I do not speak the words
that I shall never understand.
All that I can say to you is this:

chair, snow, eyelashes, lamp.

And my hands
are simple and distant,

and the window-frames
seem cut from white paper,

but there, beyond them,
around the lamp-posts,
whirls the snow

from our very childhood.

And will go on whirling while people
remember you on earth and speak with you.

And those white flakes I once
saw in reality,
and I shut my eyes, and cannot open them,
and the white sparks whirl,

and I am not able
to stop them.

1959–60

ТИШИНА

Как будто
сквозь кровавые ветки
пробираешься к свету.

И даже сны здесь похожи
на сеть сухожилий.

Что же поделаешь, мы на земле
играем в людей.

А там –
убежища облаков,
и перегородки
снов бога,
и наша тишина, нарушенная нами,

тем, что где-то на дне
мы ее сделали
видимой и слышимой.

И мы здесь говорим голосами
и зримы оттенками,
но никто не услышит
наши подлинные голоса,

и, став самым чистым цветом,
мы не узнаем друг друга.

1960

QUIETNESS

As if
through bloody branches
you clamber towards light.

And here even dreams resemble
a network of sinews.

It can't be helped, on earth
we play at people.

But there –
are the refuges of cloud,
and partitions
of god's dreams,
and our quietness, that we shattered,

since somewhere in the depths
we made it become
visible, audible.

And here we speak with voices
and are seen in shades of colour,
but no-one will hear
our authentic voices,

and becoming purest colour,
we shall not know one another.

1960

СМЕРТЬ

Не снимая платка с головы,
умирает мама,
и единственный раз
я плачу от жалкого вида

ее домотканого платья.

О, как тихи снега,
словно их выровняли
крылья вчерашнего демона,

о, как богаты сугробы,
как будто под ними –
горы языческих

жертвоприношений.

А снежинки
все несут и несут на землю

иероглифы бога...

1960

DEATH

Not taking the scarf from her head,
mother is dying,
and for the only time
I weep at the pitiful sight

of her home-woven dress.

Oh, how quiet the snows,
as if smoothed by the wings
of yesterday's demon.

Oh, how rich the drifts,
as if they concealed
mountains of heathen

sacrificial offerings.

But the snowflakes
keep carrying carrying earthwards

the hieroglyphs of god...

1960

ДЕТСТВО

Желтая вода
на скотном дворе –
далека, холодна, априорна,

и там, как барабанные палочки,
не знают конца
алфавиты диких детей:

о Соломинка, Щепка, Осколок Стекла,
о Линейные Скифские Ветры,
и, словно карнавальная драка в подвалах,
Бумага, Бумага, Бумага,

о юнги соломинок,
о мокрые буквы на пальцах!

ЗДЕСЬ И ТЕПЕРЬ – ЭТО КАК БЫ РЕЖЕТ,
НО ТОЛЬКО МЕНЯ, НЕ ВАС!
РЕЖЕТ – ЧЕРЕЗ КАРТИНЫ И ПЛАТЬЯ
И ЧЕРЕЗ КОГТИ ПТИЦ!

Коровьи копыта – ярки, неимоверны,
что-то – от въезда в бухту,
что-то – от бала,

и сразу, как стучащие рельсы,
ярки, широки, беспощадны
обнимающие нас соучастники –
руки, сестры, шеи, мамы!

Разгуляемся снова, разгуляемся,
снова заснем и пройдем
не вчера, не сегодня, не завтра, а-а-а-а-а ! –

СКВОЗЬ КРИКИ ДЕТЕЙ,
ЧЕРЕЗ МОКРЫЕ БУКВЫ,
ЧЕРЕЗ КАРТИНЫ И ПЛАТЬЯ
И ЧЕРЕЗ КОГТИ ПТИЦ!

1960

CHILDHOOD

Yellow water
in the stockyard –
far away and cold, a priori,

and there, like drumsticks,
alphabets without end
of untamed children:

oh! Broken Glass, Splinter and Straw,
oh! Linear Scythian Winds,
and like carnival scuffles in cellars,
Paper and Paper and Paper,

oh! ship's boys of straw,
oh! damp of letters on fingers!

HERE AND NOW – IT SEEMS TO CUT,
BUT ONLY ME, NOT YOU!
CUTTING – THROUGH PICTURES AND DRESSES
AND CLAWS OF BIRDS!

Cows' hooves are bright, unbelievable,
like sailing into a bay,
or like a dance,

and then, like the pounding of rails,
bright and wide and unsparing
the embrace of those who were with us –
hands, sisters, necks, mothers!

let us breathe again, let us breathe,
let us sleep again and pass
not yesterday, today or tomorrow, o-o-o-o-o! –

THROUGH CHILDREN'S SHOUTS,
THROUGH DAMP OF LETTERS,
THROUGH PICTURES AND DRESSES
AND CLAWS OF BIRDS!

1960

УТРО В ДЕТСТВЕ

а, колебало, а,
впервые просто чисто
и озаряло без себя
и узко, одиноко

и выявлялась: полевая!
проста, русалочка!

и лилия была, как слог второй была –
на хруст мороза, –
с поверхности блестящей, мокрой,

– царапинки! – заговорю, – царапинки!

с мороза,
и на руке –
впервые след пореза

а этот плач средь трав:
– я богу отдан заново!

а нищий брат, мой ангел под зарей! –
уже тогда задумали,

чтоб объяснил,
и чтоб ушел,
и чтоб осталась эта суть:
царапинки… заговорю – царапинки…

1961

MORNING IN CHILDHOOD

a, it rocked, a,
for the first time simple pure
and was lighting apart from itself
narrowly, alone

and she was there: from the fields!
simple, a little mermaid!

and a lily was there, was like a second syllable –
on to crunch of frost, –
from the shining damp surface,

– little scratches! – I shall say – little scratches!

out of the frost,
and on the hand –
for the first time the mark of a cut

and these tears among grasses:
– again I am given to god!

but beggarly brother, my angel beneath the dawn! –
even then they had planned

that I should explain,
and that I should leave,
and this essence remain:
little scratches... I shall say – little scratches...

1961

ЗАМОРСКАЯ ПТИЦА

А. Волконскому

отсвет невидимый птичьего образа
ранит в тревоге живущего друга

и это никем из людей не колеблемо
словно в системе земли
сила соловья создающая
словно в словах исключение смерти:
сердце – сечение – север

а рядом приход и уход
замечающих перья и когти
знающих гвозди крюки и столбы
не боящихся видеть друг друга

и надо на улице утром на шею принять
холод от стен и сугробов
и тайная фраза синичья
диктует сердечную славу всему

слава белому цвету – присутствию бога
в его тайнике для сомнений
слава бедной столице и светлому нищенству века

снегам – рассекающим – сутью бесцветья
бога – лицо

светлому – ангелу – страха
цвета – лица – серебра

1962

BIRD FROM BEYOND THE SEAS

to Andrey Volkonsky

reflection unseen of a bird's image
wounds the heart of my anxious friend

and it is not to be shaken by man
as if in the system of earth
the power of the nightingale creating
as in words the exclusion of death
heart – hurt – north

but nearby the coming and going
of those who see feathers and claws
who know nails hooks and posts
and do not fear seeing each other

and in the street early the neck has to take
cold from walls and from snowdrifts
and the blue-tit's secret phrase
dictates heart's praise to all things

praise to the colour white – god's presence
in his refuge for doubts
praise to the poor city the bright and beggarly age

to snows – that cut – with essence of colourlessness
the face – of god

to the bright – angel – of fear
of colour – of face – of silver

1962

КАЗИМИР МАЛЕВИЧ

> ...и восходят поля в небо.
> *Из песнопения (вариант)*

где сторож труда только образ Отца
не введено поклонение кругу
и доски простые не требуют лика

а издали – будто бы пение церкви
не знает отныне певцов-восприемников
и построено словно не знавший
периодов времени город

так же и воля другая в те годы творила
себя же самой расстановку –
город – страница – железо – поляна – квадрат:

– прост как огонь под золой утешающий Витебск

– под знаком намека был отдан и взят Велимир

– а Эль он как линия он вдалеке для прощанья

– это как будто концовка для Библии: срез – завершение –
                                                    Хармс

– в досках другими исполнен
белого гроба эскиз

и – восходят – поля – в небо
от каждого – есть – направление
к каждой – звезде

и бьет управляя железа концом
под нищей зарей
и круг завершился: как с неба увидена
работа чтоб видеть как с неба

1962

KAZIMIR MALEVICH

> ... and the fields go up to heaven.
> *From a variant of the liturgy*

where the one guardian of work is the Father's image
there is no bowing to the circle
and plain boards call for no holy face

but from far off it seems the church's singing
henceforth knows no godparent-singers
and is built in the form of a city
unfamiliar with periods of time

so too in those years another will was creating
an order of its own self
city – page – iron – clearing – rectangle:

– simple as fire under ashes consoling Vitebsk

– in the sign of allusion Velimir was surrendered and seized

– but El he is like a line he is distant for leavetaking

– it seems a colophon for the Bible: cut – conclusion – Kharms

– on boards by others is completed
the sketch of a white coffin

and – the fields – go up – to heaven
from each – there is – a direction
to every – star

and wielding the iron end it beats
under the beggarly dawn
and the circle is closed: as if from heaven is seen
work to see as from heaven

1962

УТРО В АВГУСТЕ

прячем день от себя замечая невольно
словно в горнице листья в саду
и таится он мирно
где-то в этом же доме где дети играют –
от нас независимо
мы не при чем

пусть тебя создает этот свет выявляя подробно
отпечаток тем временем примут
уходящие всегда навсегда:

все окна и двери открыты везде постоянно
рвут ветки свет
от колебанья межсвета единого
страдания в нас
и того что над нами

за которым хранится давно
отсвет робкого облика
в самой глубине первосвета

1963

MORNING IN AUGUST

we hide day from ourselves yet cannot help seeing
as if in a chamber the leaves in the garden
and quietly it hides
somewhere in this very house where the children are playing –
independent of us
no business of ours

may this light create you showing forth each detail
its imprint will meanwhile descend
on those who leave always for ever:

all windows and doors are everywhere open unceasingly
and branches pluck light
from the trembling of single midlight
of suffering in us
and of what is above us

and behind it has long been preserved
reflection of shy features
in the depth of firstlight

1963

РЕКА ЗА ГОРОДОМ

а паутинная
пылью со дна как местами чердачными
восходящая к полю

и шелк и паутина
ее притягивая увлекутся
соседями оказаться такими же
как тень и пыль

и паутинная
как шелк во сне покажется нездешней
и связи с облаками
из пуха-хромоножки трав
глаза обманывающих

и алеющих

1964

RIVER OUTSIDE TOWN

and gossamer-like
like dust from its bed as in attic places
it goes up to the field

and gossamer and silk
will be led as they draw it towards them
to be neighbours as good
as shadow and dust

and gossamer-like
as silk in sleep it will seem to be not of this place
and the lines to the clouds
are of cripple-down and of grasses
that deceive the eye

and flush scarlet

1964

ЗАСЫПАЮЩИЙ В ДЕТСТВЕ

а высоко – река моя из ду́хов:
друг в друга вы вбегающие
и так – темнея –
вдаль и вдаль

и от ушибов дела нежащего
любимые и мягкие
вы платья странны в той реке:

не детского ли духа искрами
там в черной дали голубой

а сами – прорубями в свете открывающемся
вы в свете поля далеко мелькающие
как над полянами в лесу – их лики:

вы где-то в поле на ветру
как рукопись теперь во сне – его поверхностью белеющей:

– светлы́

1965

ONE GOING TO SLEEP IN CHILDHOOD

but high up – my river of spirits:
you running each into other
and thus – growing dark –
far off and far off

and from bruises of cherishing
beloved and soft
you dresses are strange in that river:

could it be in sparks of child spirit
there in the black blue distance

and – like water holes in opening light
you flicker far off in the light of the field
as over forest clearings – their holy faces:

you somewhere in the field in the wind
like a manuscript now in sleep – with whitening surface:

are bright

1965

НОЧЬ К ВЕСНЕ

темно в сенях
в одежде есть пугающее
от дерева ли зверя ли какого
пылающими островками
опасное для разума плывет

петух отметит криком оползень
далекого комка земли
и тьма хранит свои столбы и впадины
огнем неведомым притянутые издали

чтоб место белым дать полям
края поляны затенить

1964

NIGHT TOWARDS SPRING

it is dark in the hall
in clothes there is something scaring
from a tree could it be or some beast
in flaming islets
danger to reason comes swimming

the cock will mark with a shout the slipping
of a distant clod of earth
and the dark keeps its pillars and dents
dragged by unknown fire from afar

to make room for the fields of white
to darken the clearing's edges

1964

К ПОСВЯЩЕНИЮ ДЕТСТВА:
ЧИСТКА ОРЕХОВ

> Розоволокотные, чистые…
> *Сафо*

о р о з о в о л о к о т н ы е! –

стаей простой:

на срубе
ореховы чистите гранки –

от зерен
и глади дорог
отражаясь:

как легкие дольки:

совместны!.. чисты –

о настолько! – что кажется: э т о м у   долго
как звукоряду:

свободно простукивать:

над полем
над срубом:

воздушными косточками! –

словно на память – о бывшем когда-то:

стройном и чистом:

устройстве вещей

1964

FOR DEDICATION OF CHILDHOOD:
CLEANING WALNUTS

> Red-elbowed, pure...
> *Sappho*

oh *red-elbowed ones*! –

a simple flock!

on the logs
you are cleaning walnut pieces –

reflected
from kernels
and smoothness of roads:

like the light segments:

belonging together!... pure –

oh so pure! – that it seems: *this* must
like a long scale of sounds:

freely drum out:

over field
over logs:

like knuckle-bones of air! –

as if in memory – of a once existing:

shapely and pure

order of things

1964

ЗАРЯ: В ПЕРЕРЫВАХ СНА

где *есмь* как золотую пыль –

как обрамленье красное приснившееся книги:
"néant de voix" –

от сердца высоко во сне над ним висящее –

о так сжигают *есмь:*

и жизнь – как некою его: умершею! –

она – разрозненною красною
как в плаче перерывы
мои теперь со сна! –

и лишь сознанье где-то сплавом ангельским
над тенью здесь затерянной –

иное
далеко

1965

DAWN: IN THE INTERVALS OF SLEEP

where the *I am* like golden dust –

like the red frame dreamed of a book:
"néant de voix" –

hanging high above him in sleep from the heart –

is burnt oh so it is burnt:

and life is like something of his: something dead! –

it is separated and red
like the intervals of weeping
mine now from sleep! –

and only consciousness somewhere in angelic fusion
above the shade here lost

is other
distant

1965

ДОМ ПОЭТА В ВОЛОГДЕ

(Константин Батюшков)

Любезный образ в душу налетал...
П. Вяземский

а рядом – шёлка окружение:

разорванного будто в смеси –

сияния его
и дрожи:

непрекращаемой: виска –

лицо меняющей
как в ветре –

в сияньи шёлка – словно облика:

из праха! –

сущего:

всего –

из окон ветром разъедаемого:

и светом: до лица живого –

таящегося
как драгоценность:

средь шёлка:

ветра:

и лучей

1966

HOUSE OF THE POET IN VOLOGDA

(Konstantin Batyushkov)

> The charming image visited my soul....
> *P. Vyazemsky*

but alongside – surrounding of silk:

as if torn in a mixture –

of its shining
and trembling:

unceasing: of the temple –

altering the face
as in the wind –

in the shining of silk – as of features:

out of dust! –

of everything:

that is –

corroded by wind from the windows:

and by light: to the living face –

concealing itself
like a treasure:

amidst the silk:

the wind:

and the rays

1966

РОЗЫ В АВГУСТЕ

> ...Это было поздним летом
> Меж ракит и на песке.
> *И. Анненский*

о как
боляще – без границ! –
вы близки нам в провалах ваших тлеющих:

как в наших чувствах –
кость лица! –

как будто
в близости вы той
когда в любимой умирающей
слепя мерещится нам бездна –

и в лица входит
разрушая
сырая дробность
белизны

1966

ROSES IN AUGUST

> ... It was in late summer
> Among willows and on sand.
> *I. Annensky*

oh you
how painfully – without limits! –
close to us in your smouldering collapse:

as in our feelings –
bone of the face! –

as if you
were in that closeness
when in a loved woman dying
blinded we glimpse the pit –

and into faces
destroying comes
damp fracturation
of whiteness

1966

И: ОТЦВЕТАЮТ РОЗЫ

нет спящего – а есть приснившееся!

подобно
пламени трепещущему!

и одиноко:

до провала:

его – никем не ощущаемого –

до бездны –
меры не имеющей:

гореть вещам
незримых мест:

основе
место уступая
всего:

и праха:

и души:

так: рассыпа́л бы я с себя!

так: "Эли! Эли!.." не было бы сказано!

так: розы были

так:

их нет

1966

AND: THE ROSES LOSE THEIR PETALS

there is no sleeper – but there is the dreamed!

resembling
a quivering flame!

and solitary:

to the collapse:

of it – unperceived by all –

to the abyss –
that knows no measure:

things of unseen places
will burn:

giving way
to the ground
of all:

both of dust:

and of soul:

so: I should scatter from myself!

so: "Eli! Eli!..." would not be spoken!

so: roses were

so:

they are not

1966

РОЗЫ С КОНЦА

и уступаете вы место
дальнейшему:

уже незримому

тому
чей трепет обособлен
чего и воздух не коснется

чему не содержаться в мире
в пыли движения
и времени

и ради торжества которого
заранее
распад задуман

и вашей белизны самой

1966

ROSES FROM THE END

and you make room
for the subsequent:

the already unseen

that
whose tremor is apart
which even air cannot touch

which cannot be contained in the world
in the dust of movement
and time

for the sake of whose triumph
was conceived in advance
the scattering

even of your whiteness itself

1966

СОН: ДОРОГА В ПОЛЕ

зачем тебе – почти несуществующему
искать другого –

праха не имеющего?.. –

что от дороги примешь? тень ее
содержит что-то...

пищу неземную:

не там она... тебе не обнаружить
следов того –

кто раньше посетил...

1967

DREAM: ROAD IN THE FIELD

why should you – so close to not being
seek that other –

without mortal dust?... –

what will you take from the road? its shadow
holds something...

food not of this earth:

not there its place... not yours to find
traces of him –

who earlier trod this place...

1967

К РАЗГОВОРУ О К. – ОЛЬГЕ МАШКОВОЙ

земля лишь мысль – свободно посещающая:

меняющаяся:

иногда известная
мне мыслью – Прагой:

и тогда я вижу
могилу в городе –

она – как горе-мысль:

земля – страдания!.. его – как мысли той
которая теперь так постоянна!..

скажу о той могиле "сон":

и – как не верим яви мы при ранах –

он – словно снящийся
другому сну:

как будто нескончаемому:

мне

1967

FOR A CONVERSATION ABOUT K. – TO OLGA MASHKOVA

earth is just a thought – freely visiting:

changing:

sometimes known to me
in a thought that is Prague:

and then I see
a grave in the city –

it is like a grief-thought:

earth – of suffering!... his – as of that thought
which is now so constant!...

I shall say of that grave "a dream":

and – as even wounds do not make us believe it is real –

he seems dreamed
in another sleep:

as if unending:

by me

1967

УТЕШЕНИЕ: ПОЛЕ

в образе – в прахе (как в облаке алом):

поля (как в зареве):

поля (как духа):

ты пребывай
о молитва (бессонница) –

словно окрашиваясь! –

радуя (слабого):

(о из огня его:

долго:

до грусти!) –

словно в соборе! –

свободно окрашиваясь:

(зная что будет):

и мысль не приемлющее! –

вечно (как ветер – собор бесконечный):

о независимо!
(ибо без праха):

без столкновения:

поле (как дух)

1967

CONSOLATION: FIELD

in the image – in the dust (as in a scarlet cloud):

of a field (as in sky-glow):

of a field (as of spirit):

abide
oh prayer (insomnia) –

as if taking colour! –

gladdening (the weak):

(oh from its fire:

long:

unto sadness!) –

as if in communion! –

freely taking colour:

(knowing what will be):

not accepting the thought! –

eternally (like wind – infinite communion):

oh independently!
(because without dust):

without collision:

field (like spirit)

1967

ПОЛЕ ЗА ФЕРАПОНТОВЫМ

И.М.

о небо-окно!.. –

о в далекое
чистое
окно сотворенное:

ветр – до земли – сквозь короны светил:

без шума
без веса:

в поляну-окно! –

и сосуда прозрачно-холодного
в отверстие – веянье:

в   о к н о   человека
(над полем по полю):

в чистую Чашу
ума-восприятия!.. –

и – в довершение мира соборно-сияющего:

творящее Смысло-Веленье свое
(Разговору подобное)
Светоналичностью:

ветр-озаренье! – из солнца-окна удаляющегося:

в ясное:

незамутненное:

поле-окно

1967

FIELD NEAR FERAPONTOVO

to I.M.

oh heaven-window!... –

oh into the distant
window
pure and created:

wind – to earth – through crowns of stars:

without noise
without weight:

into the window-clearing! –

into the transparent-cool vessel's
opening – the breath wafted:

into the *window* of man
(over field through field):

into the pure Cup
of mind-perception!... –

and – completing the together-shining world:

creating its Meaning-Commandment
(resembling Conversation)
with Lightpresence:

wind-illumination! – from sun-window moving away:

into the clear:

limpid-untroubled:

field-window

1967

БЕЛЫЙ ШИПОВНИК В ГОРАХ

кто озвучивал белое?
флейтой какою?
кого проявляешь – сияя?.. –

. . . . –

ты –   с о н   м у х а м м а д а ... – а было начало его – как
                  детей той страны что душою давно уже избрана
трепет духовный!.. – детей:

Белокостных:

Опор – на равнинах!.. – и словно пронизанных
гласными – полости солнца подобными! –

и – длится он явно:

с о н   м у х а м м а д а!.. –

есть он – в горах! – пребывает в горах продолженьем его
и его глубиною:

белого – в высшем накале –   с а м а Белизна! –

не до-увидеть – не только глазами:

но и души чистотою:

пламенем высшим – уже и не жгущим! –
ее отрешенности

1969

WHITE DOGROSE IN THE MOUNTAINS

who gave sound to white?
with what flute?
whom do you show forth – shining? ... –

. . . . –

you are *dream of Muhammed*... – but its beginning was like
                        trembling of spirit of children in that country
which the soul long ago elected! ... – of children:

Whiteboned:

of Ramparts – on the plains!... – and as if shot through
with vowels – resembling the hollow of the sun! –

and – clearly it continues:

the *dream of Muhammed*! ... –

it is – in the mountains! – it abides in the mountains as the
                                                    continuation
and depth:

of white – in supreme incandescence – Whiteness *itself*! –

there is no fore-vision – not only with eyes:

but even with purity of soul:

in the highest flame – already beyond burning! –
of its non-presence

1969

ПОЛЕ: В РАЗГАРЕ ЗИМЫ

Рене Шару

бого-костер! – это чистое поле
все пропуская насквозь (и столбы верстовые и ветер и точки
     далекие мельниц: все более – будто из этого мира –
     как не наяву – удаляющиеся: о все это – искры – не
     рвущие пламя костра не-вселенского)
есмь – без следов от чего бы то ни было
не по-вселенски сияющий
бого-костер

1970

FIELD: IN THE FULL BLAZE OF WINTER

to René Char

god-pyre! – this open field
letting all things pass through (mile-posts and wind and distant
        specks of mills: all more and more – as if from this
        world – not in waking – gathering distance: oh all these
        are sparks – not rending the flame of the pyre-that-is-
        not-of-this-universe)
"I am" – without trace of anything whatever
not-of-this-universe shining
god-pyre

1970

СНОВА: ВОЗВРАЩЕНИЕ СТРАХА

К. Богатыреву

друг
мы секунду в ночном пробуждении знаем
подобную
камере яркой! –

где вздрагиваем:

словно поверхностью страха вещественного:

лицом! – уже ставшим как место где род погибает! о так оно
  развито друг мой у нас! это – чувство само: о когда же
  прорвавшись за лица – как в Зарево-Душу – и точку
  сознанья-любви расщепляя – проявится То что за
  Жизнью-как-вещью? –

когда ослепят
и разрушат:

в ы с ш е е   з р е н ь е   того-что-я-Есмь:

огромным как эта страна окончательная
ярким и не-отводимым
такой напряженности холодом – Духу подобным:

как сущностью Этого Места? –

когда же
глубинам х р а н и л и щ а с т р а х а
исток его – будто идею таящий! – раскроется:

сжигая я-Мысль! –

до дна иегового

1971

AGAIN: RETURN OF TERROR

to K. Bogatyryov

friend
we know a second in midnight waking
resembling
a brilliant cell! –

where we shudder:

as with surface of material terror! –

with the face! – already become like the place where the race
        expires! oh my friend how sensitive it is! it is feeling itself:
        oh when bursting through beyond faces – as in Skyglow-
        Soul – and splintering the point of consciousness-love
        – will That which is behind Life-as-a-thing appear? –

when they will blind
and destroy:

the *highest vision* I-am-that-I-am:

with cold so tense – resembling Spirit –
immense as that ultimate land
brilliant and inescapable:

as with essence of That Place? –

when its origin –
as if hiding the idea! – is opened
to the *deep reservoirs* of fear:

burning the I-Thought! –

to depths of Jahweh

1971

НОЧЬЮ: ВЗДРАГИВАЯ

А.М.

Ночью, внезапно,
вижу я, вздрагивая, – между лицом и подушкой –
лицо похороненного друга:
оно – как бумага оберточная (содержимое вынули):
черты – как сгибы … не вынести этих следов
исковерканных!.. –
безжизненно горе само! – все – как будто из вещи –
все более мертвой… –
и боль отменима – бесследно – лишь новою болью:
ее неживой очередностью!.. –
существованье – как действие? – скомканья – словно
рассчитанного!.. –
"всё" – как понятие? – есть – как обертка!.. – чтобы
шуршать и коверкаться …

1971

AT NIGHT: SHUDDERING

to A.M.

at Night, unexpectedly,
I see, shuddering, – between pillow and face – the face
of a buried friend:
it is – like wrapping paper (the contents removed):
features – like folds ... unbearable these mutilated
traces! ... –
grief itself unliving! – all – seems made of a thing – that
is more and more dead... –
and pain is abolished – no trace – by new pain only: its
lifeless successiveness! ... –
existence – like an action? – of crumpling – as if
calculated! ... –
"all" – like a concept? – is – like a wrapping! ... – to
rustle and be mutilated...

1971

ПОЛЕ: ТУМАН

Сестре Еве

а сердце проваливается! – вдруг – представляются мне
                                        состоянья тумана:

определенья – как счастье и горе просты:

т у м а н – лишь "люблю":

з а д е в а е т   о н   с р у б – ("душу б отдал за это!"):

ж н и в ь е   у в л а ж н я е т – ("оплакиваю"):

с т е л е т с я – ("плачу… – как будто прощаюсь всю жизнь я с
            Родимой и Нищей в родимо-печальном ее одеяньи:
            всегда – навсегда – домотканом:
с болью оплакивая
уже навсегда – в состоянии этом"):

"плачу" – (и стелется – так же родимо – и одиноко – туман)

1971

FIELD: MIST

to my sister Eva

but the heart fails! – suddenly – I see the states of mist:

definitions – like grief and happiness simple:

mist – merely "I love":

it touches the woodpile – ("I would give my soul for this!"):

it dampens the stubble – ("I mourn"):

it spreads – ("I weep… – as if all my life I were saying goodbye
              to the Dear and the Poor one in her dear-sad dress: for
              ever – and ever – homespun:
mourning with pain
already for ever – in this state"):

"I weep" – (and it spreads – just as dear – and as lonely – the mist)

1971

ТЫ – ЛИКАМИ ЦВЕТОВ

Господь, Ты – ликами цветов на том –
раскрывшемся мне – свете
    самих цветов!..
    (О, как бело, пугающе! – как память о белизне
отхоже-яркого!)
    И вглядывается душа:
    вот – крест-цветок и циферблат-цветок, цветок-
часовня и цветок-собор и – Господи! – цветок-"я"-Мертвое –
в себя (пока живого) всматривающийся.
    И – отступи, душа, пред самым страшным,
    сияющим, все концентрируя,
    сияющим, как будто властным
    все исчерпать, приняв в себя! –
(еще немного – и меня всего!).
    Не вымолви, душа: "Господь-цветок",
    чтоб не успела Смерть раскрыться в нем.

1972

THOU – IN FACES OF FLOWERS

Lord, Thou – in faces of flowers in that – revealed to
me – light
of flowers themselves!...
(Oh, how white, frighteningly! – like remembered
whiteness of what is departingly-bright!)
And the soul stares in:
here are cross-flower and dial-flower, flower-chapel and
flower-cathedral and – Lord! – the flower-"I"-dead – peering
into itself (still living).
And – retreat, soul, before the most terrible,
shining, concentrating all things,
shining, as if with power
to exhaust all things and absorb them! –
(yet a little – all of me also!).
Soul, do not declare: "Lord-flower",
lest Death have time to unfold in it.

1972

ТЫ МОЯ ТИШИНА

о тебе говорю
я окраинным звездам прозрачной зимы: "о как можно
быть такой тишиною?.. " –
ею – может быть – я окружен как безмолвием поля
                              с мерцаньем участливо-ясным
но не очиститься
душе моей зыбью ее и волнами неслышными
как проясняется сон мой – как будто давно – без меня – уже
                              бодрствующий
приснившейся в этом году белизною
такой милосердною – к миру... –
но когда-то – возможно – убудет и цельность твоя и твоя
                              полнота неколеблемая
столь простая и ясная как благодать
хоть на каплю слезы за меня
и когда я исчезну – ты выскажешь горе
без слов – только отблеском горя
а взамен – словно вздох – примешь чистую долю
и стойкую меру
такой пустоты что и жизненной будет и смертной
словно там где не может быть Духа
пребывает Его утешенье... –
но – люблю я и знаю: для Бога нетронутой
сохранится твоя тишина

1974

YOU MY QUIETNESS

about you I speak
to suburban stars of transparent winter: "oh how
can such quietness be?..." –
it surrounds me – perhaps – like silence of field with glimmer
                                        compassionate-clear
but my soul cannot
be purified by its ripple and inaudible waves
as my dream is brightened – since long ago it seems – without
                                        me – already waking
by visions this year of whiteness
so charitable – to the world... –
but one day – perhaps – your wholeness too will ebb and your
                                        unshakeable fullness
as simple and clear as grace
if only by a tear shed for me
and when I am gone – you will speak out grief
without words – with a simple reflection of grief
and in return – like a sigh – will receive a pure portion
and steadfast measure
of such emptiness that it will be both of life and of death
as if where the Spirit cannot be
His consolation abides... –
but – I love and know: for God will be kept
intact your quietness

1974

МЕСТА В ЛЕСУ: ВАРИАЦИЯ

П.С. (В Казанскую психиатрическую
лечебницу специального типа.
Вместо письма)

о лес! – собор – все ввысь и вширь сияющий:

из голосов:

из м е с т в л е с у! –

и золотом
Убежища-Сокровища:

сиянием Отцовства светится:

та бесконечность Бого-Празднества!.. –

:

т а м – слух мой… –

и – двойник его:

в сиянии там чуток мой избранник:

боярышник – при пении молчащий:

как метроном божественный нетронутый
лесного целомудренного Детства! –

он – П р е б ы в а н ь я
неущербный образ:

там – только е с т ь
(не существует – б ы л о)!.. –

:

FOREST PLACES: VARIATION

to P.S. (to the Kazan special psychiatric
hospital. Instead of a letter)

oh forest! – synod – all upward outward shining:

made of voices:

of *forest-places*! –

and with gold
of Treasure-Sanctuary:

with Fatherhood's radiance shines:

that eternity of God-Festival!… –

:

there is my hearing… –

and – its double:

sensitive there in the shining my chosen one:

hawthorn – silent in the singing:

like a godly metronome untouched
of the forest's chaste Childhood! –

unwaning image
of *Abiding*:

there – there is only *being*
(*was* – no longer exists)!… –

:

и слух – не одинок!.. –

с душою-слухом
твоим
со-пребыватель   и з о л и р о в а н н ы й:

мерещится мне
в боли-озарении:

(как в золоте самом основы Торжества!):

т а м – встреча… –

словно мера неизбывности
что в нашем п р е б ы в а н и и возможна!.. –

:

(о лес!
доступность
золота Отцовства:

как мысли ясность!..) –

где-то звон его
и свеж и легок!.. –

:

(счастье-тишина)

1974

and hearing – is not alone!... –

with your
hearing-soul
fellow-abider *in isolation*:

I imagine
in pain-illumination:

(as in the very gold of Triumph!):

a meeting – *there*... –

like a measure of the permanence
that in our *abiding* is possible!... –

:

(oh forest!
accessibility
of gold of Fatherhood:

like thought's clarity!...) –

somewhere its resonance
is both fresh and light!... –

:

(happiness-quietness)

1974

ПЛАЧ-И-Я

И шел я
по теплому сору
своей же души.

(И знал: что когда-то
вели Его здесь, –

по Золоту-Морю равнины, –

средь сора тоски и страданий.)

Однородная с золотом
глина отваливалась,
когда подымался я в гору,

(я трогал руками: живая была словно песнь!),

и обрывками плача
все – в пустоте – отзывалось:

и далекие полости хижин покинутых,

и мертвых деревьев
телесное будто тепло,

и не-людская
напевность щемящая –

Золота-Глины: во всей бесконечности: Золота-Глины.

1974

WEEPING-AND-I

And I was walking
through the warm litter
of my own soul.

(And knew: that once
He was led in this place, –

over Gold-Sea of plain, –

amidst litter of sadness and sufferings.)

Of a kind with gold
clay fell away
as I climbed the hill,

(and I touched with hands: it seemed a living song!),

and in fragments of weeping
all – in emptiness – answered:

and far hollows of empty huts,

and the seeming bodily warmth
of dead trees,

and the non-human
piercing melody –

of Gold-Clay: in utter infinity: Gold-Clay.

1974

И: РОЗА-ДИТЯ

Сыну Алеше

вижу – и думаю с болью – и вследствие боли я вижу – и
                снова я думаю с болью – и снова я вижу... –

боль от любви – это длящаяся
на длительность жизни! –

это – как круг из видений и мыслей... –

это – светило из боли:

вместо огня заполняемое
болью безбрежной и неиссякаемой –

центр-озарение жизни моей:

в с е   ж е   –   б ы л о   в   б е з м о л в и и :   м е с т о
                С в о б о д ы   и   м е с т о   П о б е д ы :

и – м е с т о   Л ю б в и ! –

т и ш и н а   и   с и я н и е   с ы н а ... –

п о с л е д н я я   р о з а :

д и т я ... –

(о все видится мне: даже зубки нежны словно сердце!.. –

а свет глаз – словно песнь
на лице беспределен и неограничен)

1974

AND: A ROSE-CHILD

to my son Alyosha

I see – and with pain I think – and because of pain I see –
          and again with pain I think – and again I see... –

pain from love – continuing
while life continues! –

it is – like a circle of visions and thoughts... –

it is – a luminary of pain:

instead of fire it is filled
with boundless inexhaustible pain –

light-centre of my life:

and yet – there was in the silence: the place of Freedom and the place of
                                                              Conquest

and – the place of Love! –

quietness and shining of my son... –

a last rose:

child... –

(oh I see it all: even the little teeth tender as the heart!... –

and the light of eyes seems a song
on the face without end without limits)

1974

ШУМЯТ БЕРЕЗЫ

В. Корсунскому

и сам я – шуршащий:
“а может быть Бог…” –

шепот в березах:
“умер…” –

и мы
распад – продолжающийся? –

а почему бы
и нет? –

одиноко и пусто развеется прах… –

(шепот берез…
все мы в мире шуршим…) –

и снова
Воскреснет?.. –

… даже не больно:

как навсегда… –

шум – как об этом!.. –

. . . . –

(словно покинутый – осени шум)

1975

RUSTLE OF BIRCHES

to V. Korsunsky

and I myself – am murmuring:
"but perhaps God..." –

whisper in birches:
"is dead..." –

and we
the decay – continuing? –

and why then
should it not be so? –

lonely and empty ash will blow... –

(whisper of birches...
in this world we all murmur...) –

and will He
Rise again? ... –

... not even painful:

as if for ever... –

rustling – as of this!... –

. . . . –

(as if abandoned – autumn rustle)

1975

ТИШИНА И УЛЫБКА

о света людского
разрыв и разлет! и на каждом шагу
исчезновение
как в тайники:

страданья ли детски-особого-женского
сияния ли материнского? –

(а что говорить мне о том что мерцает бело-утаенно как
          тайное сердце всесильное нежностью и что – может
          быть – только тайна двоих?) –

и все же и все же
разрыв и разлет! –

(была эта песня земная – так скажет судьба без меня в
                    продолжении жизни с людьми) –

а боль мне такая известна
что ц в е т ее знаю!.. –

но есть – эта песня земная! –

с утра – как навек – оживление жертвенное
(о даже картавостью свето-разрывной)
пространства творимого окнами
где-то в уютном
Ненастьи-Стране... –

свеченье твое золотистое
во тьме – как в судьбе

1975

QUIETNESS AND A SMILE

oh rifts and partings
of the human world! and at every step
disappearance
as into hiding:

of childlike-most-feminine suffering
or of motherly shining? –

(and what can I say about what glimmers hidden-white like a
           secret heart all-powerful in tenderness and is only –
           perhaps – the secret of two?) –

and yet and yet
the rifts and the partings! –

(there was this song of the earth – so fate will say in my absence
                                 in continuing life with people) –

and such pain is so familiar
that I know its *colour*!... –

but it is – this song of the earth! –

from morning – as forever – sacrificial animation
(oh even with world-rending hoarseness)
of the space made by windows
somewhere in the comfort
of the Overcast-Land... –

your golden glimmer
in darkness – as in fate

1975

ПОЛЕ: МОСТ: ТРАВЫ

Г. Ю.

вздрог
проявленье

в поле в безлюдьи

(да: снова немногие да: за селом)

– немногие травы как светло-головки
где-то в свечении яви легко отдаленных
все же при сердце всегда возникающих
легких без слов сыновей… –

и обвеваю
прежней живой золотою чувствительностью:
о не развеять! – светла
и в полете – как дома! –

да вот еще: ветер! – как будто самоизлученье вселенной!.. –
                         такой беспрерывно-блистающий ветер!.. –

в открытую ясность
слуха все-ро́динного
светит – и ранит как душу:

везде обрабатывает
сиять золотистым дроблением
воздушным да в крапинках крови
(в каплях прощальных
страдания мысли прощальной) –

шири – с собою – родство
в лучах – как в сознаньи на воле
до боли родимых!.. –

:

– … да присоединяется лес своим шелестом

1975

FIELD: BRIDGE: GRASSES

to G. Yu.

shudder
revelation

in field in solitude

(yes: again not many yes: outside the village)

– just a few grasses like heads-of-light
somewhere in the waking gleam of lightly distanced
yet still in my heart appearing
light and wordless sons... –

and I breathe around them
the former living golden sensibility:
let it not be dispersed! – light
and flying – as at home! –

and again: the wind! – like selfradiance of the universe!...
                              – such continuous-sparkling wind!... –

into open clarity
of hearing all-of-motherland
it shines – and wounds as if the soul:
everywhere it is shaping
to shine with golden fracturation
of air and in speckle of blood
(in farewell drops
of the farewell thought's suffering) –

widening – with itself – the kinship
in rays – as in consciousness set free
of the painfully close!... –

:

– ... and rustling the forest joins in

1975

ЛИЦО : ТИШИНА

М. Б.

а этот вздрог наклон и спад
той темной драгоценной
(как света с тенью – скользь)
той головы (о вздрог!) –

с тенями драгоценными – лица! –

все – в говор лицевой
свободной светонадписи
все – по кости – как по частям
забра́ла лицевого тонкого! –

мельканьем световязи
как будто слышным: "Вы
уже лучом восприняты":

и света – в свете – скользь
все – чисто (скользь и ясь) –

все – пенья становленьем:

(о ме́ста вечности что есть и в нас возможно:
как встреча наша с богом:
песнь) ! –

сияньем круга: вздрог и скользь!

и – свет (вещественно – из света – счастье) ... –

сияя – одаряя – Ты
во Тьме-Стране
так ясно: долго: есть

1975

FACE: QUIETNESS

to M. B.

but this shudder inclination and fall
of that dark precious
(like slide of light with shade)
that head (oh shudder!) –

with precious shades – of face! –

all – into speech of the face
of free lightinscription
all – on bone – as on parts
of face's delicate visor! –

with flash of lightlink
seeming audible: "the ray
has already received you":

and of light – in light – the slide
all – pure (slide and clear) –

all – beginning of singing:

(oh song
of the place in eternity in us too possible:
like our meeting with god)! –

in splendour of circle: shudder and slide! –

and – light (materially – happiness – from light) ... –

shining – bestowing – You
in the Darkness-Land
so clearly: so long: You are

1975

ТАКИЕ СНЕГА

я писал бы всю жизнь
"Чистота Белизна"–
возникало б как шепот как ветр световой утешенье –
                                        прекрасное малостью:

– для себя – мне достаточно этого… –

(жизнь проходит – как будто ничья
и светла ее бедность… –

и блаженство немногое – словно проверенная
Богом – не-смертная радость:

птицы ль любой иль травы…) –

вот и видно – пора: обновленьем молитвы вернейшей шепчу я:
        "снега…" да свершится и с миром прощанье (чтоб
        без перехода у с н у л о с ь – как день завершается:
        словно Господь: без воздействия силы чьей-либо):

да скажется вздохом: "снега…":

· –

(а мир – он так просто-огромен
что даже и смерти – нам ведомой
для преображенья в неведомо-высшую
нет места иного… –

мы в нем – как умершие травы в своих семенах
                                        покрываемых снегом…):

· –

(и да остаются – как вечные…):

· –

да вздохом-душой озарится! · · · · · · · · · · · · · · · (о как же –
        должно быть – в о т с у т с т в и и страшном все-
        зе́мно чиста и едина-мгновенна
чудом – мгновенно… – душа)

1975

SUCH SNOWS

all my life I could write
"Purity Whiteness" –
like a whisper or wind of light would arise consolation – in a
                                                    mere trifle beautiful:

– for myself – this suffices... –

(life passes – like no-one's
and its poverty is bright... –

and a little blessedness – like joy not-mortal –
assayed as by God:

of a bird any bird or of grass...) –

and we see then – it is time: renewing the most true prayer I
         whisper: "snows"... let parting be done with the world
         (let *sleep* unheralded take over – as day is done: like the
         Lord: with pressure from no-one):

with a sigh be it spoken: "snows...":

. . . . –

(but the world – is so simple-immense
that even death – which we know
for transfiguration to the unfathomed highest
has no other place... –

we are in it – as dead grasses in seeds covered over by snow...):

. . . . –

(and may they remain – as eternal...):

. . . . —

and let the sigh of the soul give it light! . . . . (oh how – it
         must be – in fearful *absence* allworldly-pure and single-
         momentary
miraculously – momentarily... – the soul)

1975

И: ОБ УХОДЯЩЕМ

когда задерживается
распрощавшийся –

молчат... – лишь изредка
падают листья –

безвестья никчемная
(долго ль?)
заметность... –

в глаза не смотрят... – в застолье тихо... –

и лишь свеченьем
свободным... – чуть-чуть отстоящим:

держится (с вольным – от всех – назначеньем)
и е с м о с т ь хлеба (да им пережито
будет и место!..) и рядом –   н е м н о г о с т ь   –

вещей – притихших...

1975

AND: OF ONE DEPARTING

when having said goodbye
he lingers on –

no-one speaks... – only leaves
fall from time to time –

of absence the pointless
(but for long?)
visibility... –

no looking into eyes... – round the table quietness... –

and only in free shining... –
just a little distant:

remain (with a purpose – from all men – free)
both the *beingness* of bread (oh may the place
be lived by it too!...) and near it – the *fewness* –

of things – fallen quiet...

1975

О ДА: РОДИНА

была как лужайка страна
мир – как лужайка
там были березы-цветы
и сердце-дитя

а как те березы-цветы ветром этого мира сдувались

и розы-снега
окружали как ангелов-нищенок вздох
сельских безмолвных!.. – и с их Свето-Жалостью
вместе
светили

(здесь – место молчанью
такому же долгому
как их бесконечная жизнь)

мы назывались – *Сияния этого* многие
каждый скрепляя
свеченье живое
вторично в страданьи

(та же
и здесь
тишина)

и слушали-были: что чистота скажет Словом единым?

не прерываясь
лучилось:

мир-чистота

1975

YES: OUR MOTHERLAND

like a meadow was the country
the world – like a meadow
flower-birches were there
and heart-child

and when those flower-birches were blown away by wind
of this world

and rose-snows
surrounded unspeaking villagers like a sigh
of beggarwomen-angels!... – and with their Light-Pity
together
they shone

(here – is the place
for silence as long
as their infinite life)

we were named – of *this Shining* the many
each holding firm
the living glow

again in suffering
(here too
the self-same
quietness)

and listened: what would purity say with the single Word?

never interrupted
it radiated:

purity-world

1975

ЗАПИСЬ: APOPHATIC

К. Б.

а была бы ночь этого мира
огромна страшна как Господь-не-Открытый
такую бы надо выдерживать
но люди-убийцы
вкраплены в тьму этой ночи земной:
страшно-простая
московская страшная ночь

1976

NOTE: APOPHATIC

to K. B.

and even if the night of this world
is huge fearful like the Lord-not-Revealed
such a night must be endured
but people-assassins
stud the dark of this earthly night:
fearfully-simple
fearful Moscow night

1976

ТИШИНА

А. Хузангаю

а что он делает в лесу?
шуршит как ветка... нет бесцельнее чем ветка
и с меньшею причиной
чем от ветра... –

не знак не действие... –

и существующее в нем
лишь то – что достоянье он
Страны-Преддверья... (далее – огонь) ... –

и там
какой-то час
проявит предначертанность
конца... –

(а здешность – призрачна!.. –

и – ощущенья нет
которое
"страной" звучало) ... –

он здесь – без полноты и без молчанья леса...
лишь затиханье – прошлого... и здесь его шуршанье –
его последний признак... только – отзвук... –

(все – в пустоте... безогненной... и даже –
вселенность исключая – леса)

1975

QUIETNESS

to A. Khuzangay

but what is he doing in the forest?
rustling like a branch... more aimless than a branch
and with less cause than if
from the wind... –

not sign not action... –

and in him exists only
that he is possessed
by the Threshold-Country... (beyond it is fire)... –

and there
a certain hour
will reveal foreordaining
of the end... –

(but hereness is illusion!... –

and – there is no sensation
that might speak
of the "country")... –

he is here – without fullness or silence of the forest...
just hushing – of the past... and here his rustling –
his last apparition... just – an echo... –

(all – in emptiness... fireless... and even –
excluding the all – of the forest)

1975

ВЕТКА ВЕРБЫ В ОКНЕ

(К. Б.)

*Je ne me réveillai, transi de misère et couvert d'une
brume glacée, qu'au moment où l'on vint m'avertir que
mon meilleur ami était mort assassiné.*

Pierre Reverdy

ветка ветка
все та же
весь месяц … –

д у ш а   з о л о т и т с я
в квадрате окна!.. – а сквозь   э т о:

ВРЕЗ –

(как говорят в   и х   р е д а к ц и я х):

п е р ч а т к а – железная – чтобы – п о г л а д и т ь! –

и кровью цветет
семьи и души пронизывая
ветками гулко-внежизненными в их одиночестве
КРИК-ЧЕЛОВЕК
не имеющий эха –

(все поле мерещится поле пустое о минус-мой-друг
Боже! такой же заброшенности
мокрой как кость
такой же оставленности) –

(из яркости дня
в души просачивающаяся
тьма безущербная
с сверх-твердым беззвучием
неиссякающим) –

… о светит сегодня
одиноко по-зековски и окончательно
Кровь-Мозг
раскатами Полости – созданной наспех
тоже   с т р о и т е л ь с т в о м   и х
(и отстранение только такое
было возможно
от Быдло-Истории) –

WILLOW BRANCH AT THE WINDOW

(K. B.)

Je ne me réveillai, transi de misère et couvert d'une
brume glacée, qu'au moment où l'on vint m'avertir que
mon meilleur ami était mort assassiné.

Pierre Reverdy

the branch the branch
always the same
all the month ... –

the soul shines golden
in the window's square!... – but through *this:*

CUTTING –

(as they say *in their papers*):

a *glove* – of metal – to *stroke:* –

and in blood flowers
piercing families and souls in their solitude
with its branches resounding beyond life
a MAN-CRY
with no echo –

(I seem always to see a field an empty field oh my minus-friend
God! of such abandonment
damp as bone
of such desertedness) –

(from brightness of day
seeps into souls
unwaning dark
with over-hard silence
inexhaustible) –

... oh today there shines
lonely zek-like and ultimate
Blood-Brain
with peals of Hollowness – knocked together
by *their engineering* too
(and only such a dismissal
was possible
from Sheepish-History) –

(такими раскатами кормится
это с в е р х - М е с т о) –

... а з о л о т и т с я д у ш а и задергивается
живая
в окне... –

и чистые в днях и ночах
только ветер да свет! –

не-текущее время – застывшее поло-бесцветно
пустым монументом победы Не-жизни:

время которое высосано
до пустоты
где проклятье не действует –

(друг – знавший начало безмолвия друга) –

... тьма
я
на ощупь –

    как в поле сыром... –

("друг" – говорилось... –

друг
тьма –

друг
я
на ощупь
на шепот
на ощупь –

я
друг)

1976

(on such peals feeds
that *over-Place*) –

… but *the soul shines golden* and twitches
alive
in the window… –

and only wind and light
are pure in the days and the nights! –

unflowing time – congealed hollow-colourless
empty monument of victory of Non-life:

time that was sucked out
to emptiness
where curses do not work –

(friend – knowing the heart of friend's silence) –

… darkness
I
feeling my way –

as in a damp field… –

("friend" – was the word… –

friend
darkness –

friend
I
feeling my way
following a whisper
feeling my way –

I
friend)

1976

ТРИПТИХ С ЖАСМИНОМ

(После гибели друга)

1. ЖАСМИН – С ХОДУ

Жасмин –
как удары ножом.

И молнии мозга
в ответ.

2. СТИХОТВОРЕНИЕ-КАРТИНА

выписать тщательно меховое пальто с многочисленными
                                              каплями крови:

картину – назвать:

"ОСТАВШИЙСЯ – ПОСЛЕ УШЕДШЕГО" –

(на полу перед дверью)

3. РАЗГАР-ЦВЕТЕНЬЕ

к р о в о т о ч а щ и е   р а н ы   л ю д с к и е –
с а д ы   и х

в о з д е л ы в а т е л и – к а с т е т о м о т ы г а м и

(М о з г – Д е р н

С и я н ь е – О т е ч е с т в о)

1976

TRIPTYCH WITH JASMINE

(after the death of a friend)

1. *JASMINE – FALLING*

Jasmine –
like knife blows.

And lightning of the brain
in reply.

2. *POEM-PICTURE*

painstakingly draw a fur coat with many many drops of blood:

call – the picture:

"ONE LEFT – AFTER ONE HAS GONE" –

(on the floor outside the door)

3. *HEIGHT-OF-FLOWERING*

the bleeding wounds of humanity
are their gardens

cultivators with knuckle-duster hoes

(Brain – Turf

Radiance – Fatherland)

1976

ДРУГ МОЙ – ДЕРЕВО – ИЗ ОКНА

о старости б и одиночества
холодного стойкого! –
да только бы – с р а з у ж е!.. в м и г – в э т у
                                       н о ч ь – д о к о н ц а!
такого бы холода и одиночества
как этого дерева
простая (и даже бросаясь в глаза неприметная)
не покоримая – никем! – незаметность
мерзлость достоинство и обособленность
да непричастность (о Боже! какая
н е в о о б р а з и м а я – з д е с ь –
                                    н е п р и ч а с т н о с т ь)

1976

MY FRIEND – THE TREE – OUTSIDE

oh for old age and solitude
steadfast and cold! –
only – *at once!... this midnight – tonight – to the end!*
such coldness and solitude
as in this tree
so simply (and even while evident unnoticeably)
invincibly – by anyone – unnoticed
frozen dignified apart
and unconcerned (oh God!
unimaginably – here – unconcerned)

1976

ДА И ПОЭТ

чего не понимал
то Скукой называли
и никогда не понимал
теперь бывает: пусты дни
как будто ждет убийц и есть договоренность
и так откладывают
что скучно

и знает: то же самое у нас
не называется "трагическое"

Огромности тут нет чтобы сказать: "т а к о е"
через явления иль вещи (а вернее
упоминая куклы их – слова
как говорил Поэт другой) –

все перепутано (а впрочем равнозначно
по выстраданности):

и сына например здесь красные сапожки
пустые (жаль их)
и Солнца
подлинность Огромности

(о да
. . . .
но гимн – каркас воображаемый
оставь – и так ты знаешь)

и жаль немного: иногда
как будто пенье есть (когда: цветы)
и даже приготавливается
как за кулисами за пазухой – чтоб петься:

поэт же (анекдот: "что – Пушкин
за вас заплатит?")

да: поэт же

YES A POET TOO

what he did not understand
they called Tedium
and he never understood
sometimes now: days are empty
it seems he waits for killers and all is planned
and they put it off so long
that it is tedious

and he knows: this same thing in our country
is not called "tragic"

no Vastness here for saying: *"such a thing"*
through things or appearances (or rather
as another Poet said
by mentioning their puppets – words) –

all is confused (but still equivalent
in having suffered):

both my son's red boots for instance here
empty (and pitiful)
and the genuineness
of the Sun's Vastness

(oh yes
. . . .
but the hymn – the imagined carcass
leave it – you know it already)

and it is a little pitiful: sometimes
there seems to be singing (when there are flowers)
and even preparations
as in the wings in hiding – for singing:

a poet then (the joke: "will Pushkin
pay for you too?")

yes: a poet

(бывали – пишущие а будут – гибнущие
по-новому: без слов
и это – их Поэзия)

и выясняется
что может и повыть:
вой кукольный
и волки-куклы

(а волки-не-слова р а б о т а ю т
и будет смерть-не-слово)

теперь и в С о л н ц е – шорох есть
т р у д а такого
(и в стене – тот шорох)
шурши и сам – не забывай: "… поэт…"

какой еще глагол –
о "долге" чтоб?
а вот: струною-порванной-строкой
успей п у с т о е – в п у с т о т у:

сказать?.. – повеять словно над пожарищем
ни для чего и ни к чему?.. –

иль значиться что "был" – безгласно выдохнув
остатком пустоты и мертвизны –

что да: что есть Реальность Осиянная
(такая – для себя… – лиризм)
и нищенство-шедевр (т а к о е *есть*
что можно постучать как по железу)

1976

(at one time – they were writing but in future – perishing
a new way: wordless
and this – is their Poetry)

and it is made clear
that he can howl even:
puppet-howl
and puppet-wolves

(and wolves-not-words *work*
and death-not-word will be)

now in the *Sun* too – is a murmur
of such a *labour*
(and in the wall – that murmur)
you too must murmur – do not forget: "... a poet..."

what other word
to tell of "duty"?
this: with broken-string-verse
to speak of the *empty* –

into *emptiness:* – to waft as over flames
to no end to no purpose?... –

or to mark that "he was" – voicelessly sighing
vestige of emptiness and deathliness –

and yes: that there is Reality Illumined
(such – for the self... – is lyricism)
and the poverty-masterpiece (*such* an *is*
that we can beat as if on iron)

1976

С УТРА КУСТЫ ЖАСМИНА

а зарей собирали
из мглы островки
своей августовской торжественно-праздничной зримости –

вплавляясь все ярче испариной белой
медленно в Солнце – столь твердо незыблемо близкое
как Отчий их дом
входя в его горницу в плотницко-русском сиянии –

священнодействием

1976

JASMINE – FROM EARLY MORNING

but at dawn they gathered
out of mist little islands
of their solemnly festive August visibility

fusing ever more clearly in white exhalation
slowly into the Sun – firmly unshakenly close
like their Father's house
entering his chamber in Russian-carpenterly radiance

in a holy rite

1976

СЫНУ СЕНТЯБРЬСКИЕ ЗВЕЗДЫ

Алеше

когда сиянием не стары звезды
разноголосицей младенческою
как будто звонки в блеске –

такою чистотою родниковой
тоска лучится (через час-другой лишь ею однородною
лишь в излученьи будет Пребываемое):

Сыновьей ли назвать ее?
как будто
свободною от чувств – Земли? –

(такое что-то есть: болит как будто воздух) –

и что сказать тебе?
есть в этом для тебя
мое такое место: просто больно! –

да так – бескрайно!
будто боль разрыва
с тоской Отцовской – по-людски проходит:

сквозь душу – словно сквозь Вселенную

1976

SEPTEMBER STARS FOR MY SON

to Alyosha

when in shining the stars are not old
in childlike polyphony
as if ringing in brightness –

with such new limpid purity
sadness glows (and soon that which Abides
will be simply its singleness shining):

shall I call it Filial?
as if it were free
of the feelings – of Earth? –

(there is something of this: the air seems to ache) –

and what can I say to you?
there is for you in this
a place of mine – only pain! –

and so – without limits!
a pain as of parting
humanly passes – with Fatherly sadness:

through the soul – as if through the Universe

1976

ДОМ ЗА ГОРОДОМ

Сыну Константину

а из Родины-Жизни
иной
затаенной –

д у ш а
з о л о т и т с я
в квадрате окна:

верба
цветет –

– лепечет
младенец! –

тайная встреча (цветенье и говор) –

в той – незапятнанной – Родине

1977

СОСНЫ-С-БЕРЕЗОЙ

сквозь Бога Сосен
тень-излученье:

береза-дитя

1977

HOUSE OUTSIDE TOWN

to my son Konstantin

but of Homeland-life
other
and hidden –

the soul
shines golden
in the window's square:

the willow
is flowering –

– the baby
is lisping! –

mysterious meeting (flowering and speech) –

in that – immaculate – Homeland

1977

PINES-AND-BIRCH

through the God of Pines
a shadow-radiance

the birch-child

1977

ФЛОКСЫ: БЕЗВЕТРИЕ

так остановлен ветр
что ныне будто свет
в котором – ваш покой
и наблюдающие вы – той белизною остановленной
легчайшей в свете дня

(за вами Простота – что не сказать
такая: что – Сама)

сияньем наблюдающие
не-скрыто-не-раскрыто
а как – в толпе святого тихо сердце
и как младенца в доме целомудрие

(та чистота в глазах
что-только-чистота)

1977

PHLOXES: NO WIND

the wind is held so still
that now it seems the light
in which you are at peace
and you are the observers – with that whiteness stilled
lightest in light of day

(behind you is Simplicity – not to be spoken
such: that it is – Itself)

in radiance observing
neither-unclosed-nor-closed
but like a saint's quiet heart in the crowd
and like a child's goodness in the house

(the purity in eyes
that-is-just-purity)

1977

ТЫ-ДЕНЬ

и до сердец стрижей особо доходящий
был легок ветр – носитель счастья:

(ты сам настолько много всюду был!) –

мерцанием-молитвой за тебя
прощая
День
огромно возносился! –

в стрижах – кричала (как дитя-душа):

насквозь-недосягаемость! –

однако в ней была открытость – здесь
как будто
от луча! –

и слух был – тайно-тих… –

(в тебе – как в крике – чуткий)

1977

И: МЕСТО РЯБИНЕ

Лес – весь в пятнах крови – храм опустошенный.

(Как без птиц: без душ. Без-словье и без-звучие.)

И – у входа: вся – подобием:

Параскева-Пятница-рябина.

1977

YOU-DAY

and reaching especially the hearts of swifts
the wind was light – bearer of gladness:

(yourself you were so much in every place!)

in shimmering-and-prayer for you
forgiving
Day
reared hugely up! –

in the swifts cried (like a child-soul):

through-and-through-inaccessibility! –

yet in it there was openness – here
as if
from light! –

and hearing was – secretly-still... –

(keen – in you – as in the crying)

1977

AND: MAKE WAY FOR THE ROWAN

The forest – all in splashes of blood – a ravaged temple.

(As if without birds: without souls. No-word no-sound.)

And – at the entrance: all a likeness:

Parasceve-Good-Friday-rowan.

1977

ОБРАЗ – В ПРАЗДНИК

В день 100-летия К. С. Малевича

со знанием белого
вдали человек
по белому снегу
будто с невидимым знаменем

26 февраля 1978

BIRTHDAY IMAGE

For the centenary of K. S. Malevich

with knowledge of white
a man far off
over whiteness of snow
as with an invisible banner

26 February 1978

В ВЕТР

Было и осталось...
Я. С.

1

это вещи его и в вещах так тепло
и тепло – его шаг
и от дома его в этом мире тепло
и тепло от него
хорошо от деревьев его и уютно от трав
словно вместе сияя одним
(а как счастье мелькало мое: дуновенье ведь было такое
средь вещей как в дому)

2

я как будто в муке а ведь так хорошо
в этом холоде странно-уютно
я полою одежды укрыт в этом мире
в ожидании легком
это счастье мое как за вьюшкою здесь
и буран за селом
я не знаю других (о священно-народный
словно мама народ)

3

а теперь ведь пора (я не знаю других)
и буран среди дров как душа
да шаги как тепло а его разве нет
и любое лицо словно ветр чтоб укрыть
и страдания свет навсегда по краям
создавая ту родину в мир
(и все так же – как шорох! и место его
там где нет своего из души)

1978

INTO THE WIND

It was and it remains...
Ya. S.

1

these things are his and in things is such warmth
and the warmth is his step
and his house gives such warmth to the world
and the warmth comes from him
and happiness from his trees from grasses comfort
as if all shining together as one
(and like happiness it flashed to me: the breeze
is the same among things as in the house)

2

I seem in torment yet it is so good
in this cold there is strange comfort
in this world I am covered with the tail of a coat
in a light expectation
my happiness here as behind the flue
and the blizzard beyond the village
I know no other (oh popular-holy
like a mother people)

3

and now is the same time (I know no other)
and the blizzard among logs like a soul
and steps like warmth and he is not here
and any face like a wind to cover
and the light of suffering for ever about us
bringing into the world that homeland
(and always the same – like a rustle! and his place
where the soul has nothing from itself)

1978

"ВЕТРЫ-СИЯНЬЯ: ОТЪЕЗДЫ"

Л.-Н. и М. Рогинским

а что прошло?
снега
прошли как жизнь
Нана

какая уж ни есть зима
да будет как Свеча
с тенями нашими Свеча
мигающая в мире
земли погоды и людей-детей
Свеча-Страна такая

(какая уж ни есть
друзья)

свечением ее
прошли снега и дни
прошли пространства
память
страна прошла
друзья

и не как пламя ли
Нана
передвижение? в закатном свете друг
земля людей таких
как я-прощай
как мы
как где-то-были-мы

закат такой
Нана

все меньше все огромней
Страна-Свеча
друзья

1978

"WINDS-RADIANCE: DEPARTURES"

to L. N. and M. Roginsky

and what has passed?
the snows
have passed like life
Nana

whatever winter may be
let it be like a Candle
a Candle with our shades
twinkling in the world
of earth of weather of child-folk
such a Candle-Country

(whatever it may be
my friends)

in its shining
snows and days have passed
spaces have passed
memory
the country has passed
my friends

and is it not like a flame
Nana
the moving? in sunset light a friend
the world of such people
as I-farewell
as us
as there-we-were

such a sunset
Nana

ever smaller more immense
the Candle-Country
my friends

1978

СОН: ДРУЗЬЯ И ТЫ

Друзья и ты в их шутовской гурьбе...
Б. П.

а как же – подростком-и-взрослым-меняясь
теперь
средь живых ты рисуешь? –

знаем: уйдешь ты к с в о и м
а – рисунки: останутся? можно   п о т р о г а т ь? –

о Боже такая тоска! – да еще разговариваем
с тобой же: о т о м ч т о у й д е ш ь:

(и стезею – т о й   с а м о й?) –

и с а м   подтверждаешь (глазами я спрашиваю)
что да: что ты – смысл: неизменный! –

что – мертв...

1979

DREAM: FRIENDS AND YOU

> Friends and you in the jesting crowd...
> *B. P.*

but how – by-turns-youth-and-man
do you now
make drawings among the living? –

we know: you will go away to *your own*
but the drawings – will they stay? can we *touch* them? –

God such sadness! – yet still we can talk
with you: and *about your going:*

(by that path – *the very same?*) –

and *yourself* you confirm (with my eyes I ask)
that yes: you are the meaning: never changing! –

and – dead...

1979

ЗАВЕРШЕНИЕ: ФЛОКСЫ

Питеру Франсу

когда отверженный своей душою скудной
бреду по улице а рядом-Евхаристия
и никнет голова –
так: ваша белизна – молитвой посвященных
и не поднять мне глаз
(чтоб не было: что да: лишь видимость теперь)
и не дождаться слез (лишь смутное волненье)
как вот такой
(лишь горсточкой)
страны
как в братстве бедно-родовом завещанной
запрятанно-дрожащей
красоты

1979

CONCLUSION: PHLOXES

to Peter France

when all rejected in my barren soul
I walk the street and the-Eucharist-is-by-me
and my head sinks low –
so: your whiteness is prayer of the initiate
and I cannot lift my eyes
(let it not be that now there is only appearance)
and no tears will come (only cloudy emotion)
as of that same
(only a handful)
country
as of beauty bequeathed
in poor native brotherhood
secretly trembling

1979

ИВЫ

ивы такие: уснуть! окружиться
живым будто вздох серебром
вздрогнуть и листья узнать словно шепот в блистании
                    линий (вновь – воскрешаемый солнцем)
о мягком тумане-призреньи – слезами в миру серебрящегося
детства бесстрастного! – ивы такие: уснуть!
серым рассеяться в ртутном по верху и нежность
                              прокатывать: ту что не знали
что Духом расписывают
смертью туманят

1979

WILLOWS

such willows: to fall asleep! be surrounded
with living silver like a sigh
and shudder and recognize the leaves in the shining of lines
                    like a whisper (again – raised up by the sun)
of soft mist-caring – like tears in the world of silvery-shining
passionless childhood! – such willows: to fall asleep!
greyly be scattered in quicksilver over tops and spill down
                              tenderness: the one not known
the one painted in Spirit
and misted in death

1979

ПОЛЕ-РОССИЯ

С.Б.

вот и желаю тебе!
(счастье-молитва безмолвно)
в поле умолкнуть душою ("о Бог" говорим мы
более-сердцем: долиной
белым-блистающего
вольно
вокруг
Совершенства) о как этот ветер
даже сиянье не тронул дыханья!
огнь
неизменности
веял
заметное
все
исчезало: о будь же
там
уже очень давно
не знающим – кем улыбалось:
"лучшее Чистое – ты"

1980

FIELD-RUSSIA

to S.B.

so this I wish you!
(happiness-prayer unspoken)
in the field to fall silent in soul ("Oh God" we say
with greater-heart: a valley
of white-gleaming
freely
all around
Perfection) oh how this wind
did not touch even radiance of breath!
fire
of unchangingness
wafted
things perceptible
all
were vanishing: oh then let it
be there
for a long time now
not knowing – as whom it was smiling:
"best Purest – you"

1980

В ТУМАНЕ

полный тумана
всю ночь огород – словно сад
а за ним
в тумане-лесу за оградой
голос кукушки
как будто в всегда-утихающем-неутиханьи
в далеком народе-отце
долго
давно
мой отец
(в сонме – клубящемся
шествием-пеньем)

1980

IN THE MIST

full of mist
all night the allotment – like a garden
and beyond it
beyond the fence in mist-forest
the cuckoo's voice
as if ever-quieter-unquietness
in the distant father-people
long
and long ago
my father
(in the billowing crowd
of procession-and-singing)

1980

СНОВА – ИВЫ

Ф.Л.

вдруг
понимаю что *душу твою вспоминаю*
в тумане вдали наблюдая
подъемы теперь острова перепады вершин серебристых
ивовой рощи
спокойной
(и чем-то
"потусторонней")
и что-то "такое"
("величие"? "благоуханье"
близкой души "чистоты несказанной"?)
помню должно быть (и даже вдали вместо облика я
мыслями будто удерживаю
самый тишайший провал – только нежностью ныне
                                                клубящийся)
впрочем
это одно лишь мельканье "чего-то" из памяти
когда переходы
словно "нездешних" *красот*
юностью тою роятся
где "вечное" – будто сиротство
(незримое – нас дожидаясь)

1980

AGAIN – WILLOWS

to F.L.

suddenly
I understand *I remember your soul*
observing in mist far away
slopes now or islands or steps of the silvery summits
of a willow grove
peaceful
(and in some way
"from beyond")
and "something" what is it
("magnificence"? "fragrance"
of intimate soul of "purity unspoken"?)
I must be remembering (and even far off in place of the face
I seem to retain in my thoughts
the quietest of hollows – now swirling only with tenderness)
and besides
this is only the flicker of "something" from memory
when the crossings
of *beauties* "not of this place"
cluster in that youthfulness
where the "eternal" is like orphanhood
(the unseen – awaiting our coming)

1980

И: ШУБЕРТ

боль
о тебе
появлялась: местами просвета
в юной дубраве! как ясно душою твоею
та синева прозвучать бы могла!
"музыка" мне говорили
я слышал – когда не звучала:
моей тишиною была!
позже узнал я – за нею
светлеет тоскою такая:
словно – в ответ – проясняется
мукой: Господь наш! – и нами
в грусти просимый – для нас
в боли Своей затихает

1981

AND: SCHUBERT

pain
for you
kept coming: in intervals of sky
in the young oak-wood! how clearly
that blue might resound with your soul!
"music" they were saying
I heard it – without sound:
and it was my quietness!
later I discovered – behind it
shines in longing such music:
as if – in reply – is made clear
in torment: our Lord! – and the one
we prayed for in grief – for us
in His pain grows quiet

1981

ПЕРВАЯ НЕДЕЛЯ ДОЧЕРИ

тишина
где ребенок – неровная
будто в пределах – из ломкости светотеней: пустота! – ибо
мир Возрастает
в нем – чтобы Слушать
Себя
Полнотой

22 января 1983

НАЧАЛО "ПЕРИОДА СХОДСТВ"

а силы
встревожены рода – и веют
и кружат как ветер-и-свет – проводя по лицу
облако за облаком: все – выражения
исчезнувших лиц –

чтоб выявить чтоб утвердить – "окончательный"
облик – твой:

огнем – устоявшим в вихре! –

(не тем же ли жаром – засматриваясь – вздрагиваю:

словно – средь некого пенья? –

боль – входит как ветер)

1983, март

MY DAUGHTER'S FIRST WEEK

the quietness
where the child is – seems uneven
within limits – of fragile lightshadows: emptiness! – for the
world Grows
in her – to Listen
to Itself
in its Fullness

22 January 1983

BEGINNING OF THE "PERIOD OF LIKENESSES"

and the powers
of the race are stirred – and float
and turn like wind-and-light – carrying over the face
cloud after cloud: all – expressions
of vanished faces –

to show forth to confirm – the "definitive"
appearance – your own:

in fire – standing firm in turbulence! –

(is it not with this same heat that – peering – I shudder:

as if – amid some singing? –

pain – came in like the wind)

March 1983

ПРОДОЛЖЕНИЕ "ПЕРИОДА СХОДСТВ"

промелькивает: тень? материнская?
из глуби какой: из молчания
времени – клада забытого? сон и не сон:
свет – доходя до лица: раскрывание
кого же глубокого
со вспыхнувшей связью – белеть и темнеть подымающей
быть может и древнее поле и ветр?
грусть ли – мерцанием – в личике
блужданья-отца перво-кругом неведомым
в попытках – опять обнаружиться
в буре взыгравшейся рода?
спишь ли… – а бдительно – ширясь усиливаясь –
                                                    обще-сияние:

мукой выковываясь
где же таится он – твой
свеже-и-перво-введенный
облик – средь многих других?

1983, апрель

CONTINUATION OF THE "PERIOD OF LIKENESSES"

it flits by: a shadow? maternal?
from what depths: from unspeaking
time – from a treasure forgotten? dream and not dream:
light that reaches the face: revelation
of whom then deep down
with the flash of a bond – that perhaps calls up also
white and dark of ancient field and of wind?
or could it be grief – a gleam – in the face
of father-wandering through unknown first-circle
in attempts – to find himself again
in the turbulent storm of the race?
you sleep... – but it wakes – ever wider and stronger – the
common shining:
in pain hammered out
where then is it hiding – your
fresh-and-new-found
appearance – among many others?

April 1983

ПЕСЕНКА ВРЕМЕН ТВОИХ ПРАДЕДОВ

(Вариация на тему чувашской народной песни)

> …пить не из стакана, а из чистого
> источника.
> Бела Барток, *Кантата Профана*

бродил я в поле не было там
ни одной копны

зашел я в деревню
и не увидел
там никого

а девушки сидели
за вымытыми стеклами узеньких окон
и вязали
глазастые кружева

посмотрел я в окно и увидел
что сватают мою милую
в белое платье ее нарядили
в руку дали ей ковшик

и стоит она перед столом

я плакал качаясь
перед твоим окном
и была ты тиха –

как свеча на подоконнике
высокой церкви

"вижу" молчал я
молчал я "прощай"
родных не имея "народ" – понимал я
долго потом
"что-то было" я знал

и ничего головой не запомнил
плача щеками
в руках

1957–59

SONG FROM THE DAYS OF YOUR FOREFATHERS

(variation on the theme of a Chuvash folk-song)

> ...to drink not from a glass, but from a
> clear spring.
> Béla Bartók, *Cantata Profana*

I wandered through the field and there was
not a single haycock in it

I went into the village
and there I saw
not a soul

and the girls were sitting
behind washed panes of narrow windows
and knotting
the lace full of eyes

I looked in the window and I saw
they were betrothing my beloved
in a white dress they decked her
placed a beaker in her hand

as she stood before the table

– I wept and I rocked
outside your window
and you were quiet –

like a candle on the sill
of a lofty church

"I see" I said silently
said silently "farewell"
having no family I understood – "people"
long afterwards
"there was something" I knew

and I kept nothing in my head
weeping with my cheeks
on my hands

1957–59

РОЗЫ ТРЕХЛЕТНЕЙ ЭТЕРИ

читают

ангелы
книгу твою

когда это были раскрыты страницы?

тонут
(и ум
вот-вот
забоится)

о ветроподобие

обморок
(больше меня)
поглощаемый

1983

ROSES OF ETERI AGED THREE

angels

read
your book

and when were the pages opened?

they sink
(and the mind
any moment
will take fright)

oh windlikeness

swoon
(greater than me)
consumed

1983

ПЕСЕНКА ДЛЯ ТЕБЯ – ОБ ОТЦЕ

> Был мой отец как белый пряник.
> *Из марийской народной песни*

Был
мой отец как белый пряник,
белое
сияло
добро, –

воздухом дня
поглощаясь.

А теперь в этом воздухе
нет никого,
горница – зимою – становится полем пустынным, –

теменью дня
поглощаясь.

И снятся под утро
в поле – отцовские сани
белые как пряник,
как пряник,
только в них нет никого,

но излучается,
веет над ними
белое – то же – добро, –

грустью моей
поглощаясь.

1983

LITTLE SONG FOR YOU – ABOUT YOUR FATHER

My father was like a white spice-cake.
From a Mari folk-song

My father
was like a white spice-cake,
his goodness
shone
white, –

swallowed
by the air of the day.

And now in that air
there is no-one,
the bedchamber – in winter – becomes an empty field, –

swallowed
by the dark of the day.

And before dawn I dream
of my father's sledge in the field
white as a white spice-cake,
a spice-cake
only there is no-one in it,

but over it
shines and floats
the same – white – goodness, –

swallowed
by my grief.

1983

И: ПЕРВОЕ ПОЛУГОДИЕ

ты *крестьянский младенец* рембрандта
этим ножкам ходить по дощатому полу
падать (матери не усмотреть)
и колени подогнуты – пенью простому послушны
       (подпрыгивать – больше чем быть благодарным!
      помочь и сочувствовать)
ручки – будто берущие хлеб
(так – обнимают *любовь*)
и котенок-соперник "поставлен на место" твоим
                        повзрослением
пред миской – спокоен
а Защищающий? в этой картине
всегда в полутьме:
с трудом (для ребенка и Бога) ручным

14 июля 1983

AND: THE FIRST HALF YEAR

you are a *peasant baby* out of Rembrandt
these little feet made to walk plank floors
to fall (mother cannot see everything)
and the knees are bent – obedient to a simple song (to jump
        and skip – more than to be grateful! to help and to
        sympathize)
the little hands – as if taking bread
(even so – *love* is embraced)
and the kitten-rival "put in its place" by your growing
in front of the bowl sits quiet
and the Protector? in this picture
he is always in half-darkness
with the work (for child and for God) of his hands

14 July 1983

ЭПИЛОГ:
КОЛЫБЕЛЬНАЯ-СУВАЛКИЯ

закатилося
(*куполя куполели*):

солнышко – *лелюмай:*

алелюм каледа! –

(тихо: здесь входит
в пение – *Дéмядис:*

Божие Дерево) –

куполя куполели! –

спит – в постелюшке
дочь моя – *лелюмай! –*

алелюм каледа

14 июля 1984
Сувалкия (южная область Литвы)

EPILOGUE: SUVALKIYA LULLABY

it has set
(*kupolya kupoleli*):

the sweet sun – *lelyumay:*

alelyum kaleda! –

(quietly: here comes into
the singing – *Demyadis:*

the Tree of God) –

kupolya kupoleli! –

she sleeps – in her cot
my daughter – *lelyumay!* –

alelyum kaleda

14 July 1984
Suvalkiya, Southern Lithuania

РОЗА МОЛЧАНИЯ

Б. Шнайдерману

а сердце
теперь
или только отсутствие
в такой пустоте – словно это притихло
в ожидании
место молитвы
(чистое – пребывание – в чистом)
или – скачками побыть начинающая
боль (как возможно бывает
больно – ребенку)
слабая голо-живая
будто беспомощность
птичья

1983

ROSE OF SILENCE

to B. Schnaiderman

and the heart
now
or only absence
in such emptiness – as if hushed
in waiting
the place of prayer
(pure – abiding – in the pure)
or – pain beginning by starts
to be there (as perhaps
a child – feels pain)
weak nakedly-living
helplessness
like a bird's

1983

ПОСЛЕДНИЙ ОВРАГ

(Пауль Целан)

М. Брода

Поднимаюсь;
так строят
в хождении
храм.
Веет братство, – мы в облаке этом:
я (с незнакомым мне словом
как будто оно не в уме) и полынь (беспокойною горечью
рядом толкающая
мне это слово),
о, снова
полынь.
Глина,
сестра.
И, из смыслов, единственно бывший ненужным и главным,
здесь (в этих комьях убитых)
как имя никчемное. Им
пачкаюсь я, подымаясь
в очень простом – как огонь – озареньи,
чтобы отметиться метой последней
вместо – вершины; она
пустым (ибо все уже отдано)
лицом: будто место безболья
высится – по-над полынью.
(...
И
форма
была
не
увидена
...)
А облако:
стали слепее (безликостью полой),
дно – без движения; свет
как от разверзтости – камня.
Все более
вверх.

1983

THE LAST RAVINE

(Paul Celan)

to M. Broda

I climb;
thus in walking
one builds
a temple.
Breath of fraternity, – we are in this cloud:
I (with a word unknown to me
as if not in my mind) and wormwood (unquietly bitter
alongside me thrusting
this word on me),
oh, once more
wormwood.
Clay,
my sister.
And, of meanings, the one that was needless and central,
here (in these clods of the murdered)
seems a name to no purpose. With it
I am stained as I climb
in simple – like fire – illumination,
to be marked with a final mark
in place – of a summit; like
an empty (since all is already abandoned)
face: like a place of painlessness
it towers – above the wormwood.
(…
And
the form
was
not
seen
…)
But the cloud:
they grew blinder (in hollow facelessness),
the depths – without movement; the light
as from openedness – of stone.
Ever higher
and higher.

1983

ЛИСТОПАД И МОЛЧАНИЕ

1

Чтобы
собой я молился,
Ты
не наполняешься мне – молитвой,
и явным отсутствием
крепким
я окружен, как кру́гом.

2

А ею
ребенком – молиться
я не могу. Она
сама по себе – молитва. Ты, этим кругом тихим,
Сам
полнотою
в Себе.

3

Что́ я
в Молчаньи – как в Свете ровном?
Или в огне. А живущее – мерзлое равенство деревьев
                                         больных. И при этом – Ты,
ясность, – о, непроглядная ясность. В сравнении с нею
смерть – обещание… – что-то другое!.. И кругом мертвым
невыносимо
падает с дерева – лист.

1984

LEAF-FALL AND SILENCE

1

so that I
in myself should pray,
You
are not filled for me – with prayer,
and in evident powerful
absence
I am ringed, encircled.

2

But in her
the child – I cannot
pray. She is in herself
a prayer. You, in this quiet circle
Yourself
are utterly
in Yourself.

3

What am I
in the Silence – as in steady Light?
Or in fire. But the sick trees' frozen equality is living. And
                                        You, next to this –
are clarity, – oh, impenetrable clarity. Compared to it
death is a promise... – is something other!... And in a dead circle
unendurably
falls from a tree – a leaf.

1984

ПОЛЯНА-ПРОЩАНИЕ

T. Венцлове

пение (их же – внезапное)
их вызывало – и они вырастали – с объятьями
там – на поляне раскачиваясь
(пенье раскачивалось):
в отцы – из отцов – вырастали (и свет
отцов – раскачивался):
пели – страну находя-колыхая (тем самым теряя
ибо
теперь
уже нахожденье любое – потеря
все более – обще-Земная)
и возвращение это горело-раскачивалось:
в руках – на плечах друг у друга – пылало
прощанье! – уже нахожденье
то – окончательное
(ибо – последнее)

1984

CLEARING-FAREWELL

to T. Venzlova

singing (sudden – and theirs)
called them forth – and they grew – embracing
there – rocking in the clearing
(the singing was rocking):
into fathers – out of fathers – they grew (and light
of the fathers was rocking):
they sang – finding-waving the land (and thus losing it
because
now
any finding – is loss
ever more – Earth-wide)
and it burned this return it was rocking:
in each other's hands – and shoulders – flamed
farewell! – already the finding
is definitive
(for it is the last)

1984

ГОРЯ́ – ВО ВРЕМЕНИ ЖАТВЫ

Л. Р.

и углубляюсь я – в жатву: о этот
огонь – закалявший
терпенье отцов – как безвинность земли! – и блистала
                                                страна Простотою
будто – звенела: в ее небеса восходили
смыслоназвания
Бедных Вещей – и прозрачность их доброприсутствия
сердце ковала того кто умом отдаляясь в пределы другие
ведал – о невозвращении
в этот очаг . . . . – отзвенело давно в
                                безымянности обще-пространства
то завершение круга – отсутствием свето-основы: сиянья
                                отцов запевавших плечами
как лицами неба и почвы! – и ныне
только молчание Слова
безликостью мира блистает . . . . – а было же
                просто: ведь даже подобье шептанья несмелого
было – как личико-небо – повсюду глубокое
родное – без края

1983

BURNING – DURING HARVEST

to L. R.

I bury myself – in the harvest: oh
this fire – that once tempered
our fathers' patience – like the guiltlessness of earth! – and the
                                        Land in simplicity gleamed
as if – it was ringing: and into its heavens ascended
meaningnames
of Poor Things – and translucence of their goodpresence
forged the heart of one who inwardly leaving for other walks
knew – of non-return
to this hearth . . . . – long ago ceased ringing in
                                        anonymous common-space
that closing of the circle – in absence of light-foundation: of the
                                fathers' shining as they sang with shoulders
as with faces of sky and soil! – and today
only the silence of the Word
gleams in the facelessness of the world . . . . – yet it was
                        simple: yes even the likeness of timid whispering
was – like this heaven-face – everywhere deep
and dear – without limit

1983

ЛЕСА – ВСПЯТЬ

в тумане
сияния родины
островами остались жемчугами остались
леса до которых
я никогда не добрался –

– детское что-то я помню: то ль плечики в них выступали –
                                                белели наклонно к полям
то ли жалобой
вдруг – расслаблялось движенье: скорее в печали
чем зримое – там на опушке
недостижимой –

(были такие – я видел столь близко
а скоро
был только лишь ветер –

легко я – как в ветре – учился
легко понимать что уже не вернуться) –

в свете долин-перекрестков
казалось – что дети средь трав просыпались
и пенье искало слова – где-то рядом
будто
оттуда казалось –

в тумане сияния мира
жемчугами остались островами остались:

больнее чем в жизни – сиять

1985

FORESTS – BACKWARDS

in the mist
of the shining of home
have remained like islands like pearls
the forests
I never reached –

– I remember something of childhood: little shoulders visible in
                              them – white inclining to the fields
or else suddenly
complaining – movement slackened: more in sorrow
than the visible – there on the inaccessible
edge of the forest –

(there were some – I saw from so near
but soon
there was only the wind –

easily – as if in the wind – I learned
easily to understand that there is no return) –

in the light of valley-crossings
it seemed – that children awoke amid grasses
and their singing sought words – somewhere nearby
as if from there
it seemed –

in the mist of the shining of the world
they remained like pearls like islands:

more painfully than in life – to shine

1985

И: МЕСТО – ДАВНЕГО ЗНАКА

а то что однажды
мелькнуло – как будто виденьем:

– при свете закатном
кланяющейся головы красота –

(добром ли творилась творила ль добро) –

остается – сиять:

там – где когда-то народ
был – полем а место:

головы-излучения:

– серединою миропространства! –

(прозрачного душами – будто единым:

ветром – особым) –

о – продолжаясь:

(давно уже нет никому даже веянья дара – и видеть и
                                                          помнить) –

в мире (да хоть отмененном) средь Поля-России:

кланяющейся головы красота

1985

AND: THE PLACE – OF THE FORMER SIGN

and that which once
was glimpsed – as if in a vision:

– in sunset light
beauty of a bowed head –

(from goodness created or creating goodness) –

remains – to shine:

there – where once the people
was – a field and the place:

of head-radiance:

– centre of worldspace! –

(transparent with souls – as if with one:

special – wind) –

oh – persisting:

(there has long been for no-one even the breath of the gift –
                                        to see and remember) –

in the world (even if abolished) amidst Field-Russia

beauty of a bowed head

1985

МАКИ ЭТОГО ГОДА

а не молчание а просто вроде
когда грустим мы отвечанья:
"не мы спасаем не красота спасет
во всяком случае не наша не похожая
мы дети – можно обижать – такие
что можете войти – пройти вы как угодно
мы не задерживаем прекрасны мы по-своему
но слабые – лишь одеяние невидимого
как срока некоего
а ты ищи ты излеченья там
чего не знаем
– пройдя ли через нас? мы просто кротость
вы – сила действенная мы – цветем
лишь от прикосновения
другой неспешной благосклонной силы
и это тоже лишь часы и дни
как соловей поет
дитя
не зная двигающей мощи
а отцветают так – и отцветем
как пенья нет – а сила неподвижна
проверкой" а не веянье а вроде
грусть – в слабых спотыканьях: так над полем
туманятся – подобья

1985

POPPIES OF THIS YEAR

and not silence but to our grieving
as it were an answering:
"we are no saviours no saviour beauty
or at least not ours not our likeness
we are children – vulnerable – such
that you come in and through us freely
we do not hold you we have our beauty
but are weak – just clothing of the unseen
as of some span of time
and you – seek seek a cure there
a cure unknown to us
– passing though us? we are just meekness
you – an active force – we flower
from the merest touching
of another power unhurried benevolent
and this too is just hours and days
like a nightingale sings
a child
not knowing the impelling force
and thus they wither – and we shall wither
when the song is gone – and the power is still
and testing" and not inspiration but a kind of
grief – in weak stumbling: thus above the field
cluster – clouds of likeness

1985

СНЕГ В ПОЛДЕНЬ

Дочери, – в день ее трехлетия

"вижу люблю"– и он светел как светел
а "помню люблю я когда за окном он невидим"
тогда – он волнующе-тускл! – от все более общего
светобогатства! – и радость людская там где-то трепещет
вся – обновленная
тихим участьем: движений-волнений твоих дополненьем –

из жизни доверчиво-ясной

1986

SNOW AT MIDDAY

to my daughter – on her third birthday

"I see I love" – and it is light so light
and "I remember I love it outside the window unseen"
then – it is touchingly-dim! – from the ever more common
lighttreasure! – and human joy somewhere there quivers
all – made new
by quiet sympathy: addition of your movements-emotions –

from a life that is trusting-clear

1986

ПОСЛЕДНИЙ ОТЪЕЗД

(Валленберг в Будапеште: 1988)

Впервые выпущенный за границу, лето 1988 года я провел в Будапеште.

Я давно интересовался выдающимся венгерским ваятелем Имре Варгой (особенно запомнилось мне, по журнальной репродукции, скульптурное изображение поэта-мученика, узника гитлеровских концлагерей Миклоша Радноти, которого я переводил на чувашский язык).

Будапештские друзья в первые же дни повезли меня осмотреть памятник Раулю Валленбергу, сооруженный в мае 1987 года по проекту Варги. Потом я часто сиживал в маленьком скверике, где стоит бронзовый Валленберг, и весь последующий месяц, не определив еще жанра, писал захватившую меня вещь, – даже во время длительных, утомительных путешествий по стране.

Первоначальным заглавием сочиняемого было – "Рука Валленберга", – странно-загадочный, остановленно- "движущийся" жест этой руки неотвязно вторгался в мои черновики. Спустя год, я стал подбирать эпиграф к завершенной маленькой поэме, обратился для этого к религиозной литературе: как, теологически, определяется Рука – "орган и знак действия, выражения, связи". Градации ее определения оказались обширными: от "власти" и "обладания" – до "отпускания" и "утешения", все это, – как мне все более вспоминалось, – было в замечательном творении Варги.

"Сын Десницы" – "тайно", лишь про себя, называл я великого шведа (есть и такое определение избранников Господа, именуемого также "Мужем Десницы"), но название поэмы и эпиграф я выбрал – более соответствующие безмолвной, сдержанной жертвенности Рауля Валленберга.

В заключение хочу отметить, что слова *Хайя* и *Аум* взяты из рефренов еврейских колыбельных песен.

Январь 1991

FINAL DEPARTURE

(Wallenberg in Budapest: 1988)

In 1988, when I was allowed abroad for the first time, I spent the summer in Budapest.

I had long been interested in the outstanding Hungarian sculptor Imre Varga – I had retained a particularly strong memory of a newspaper reproduction of a sculpture of the poet-martyr Miklós Radnóti, a victim of Hitler's concentration camps, whom I had translated into Chuvash.

On one of the first days after my arrival, my Budapest friends took me to see the monument to Raoul Wallenberg, erected in May 1987 to a design by Varga. Thereafter, I often used to sit in the little park where the bronze Wallenberg stands, and all the following month, not yet knowing what kind of work it would be, I worked on a subject that would not leave me in peace, even during long and tiring journeys all over Hungary.

The initial title of what I was writing was "Wallenberg's Hand" – the strangely enigmatic, stationary yet "moving" gesture of that hand kept finding its way into my rough drafts. A year later I began to look for an epigraph for the poem I had completed, and turned to religious literature. In theology the Hand is defined as "the instrument and sign of action, expression, communication". The levels of meaning turned out to cover an enormous range: from "power" and "possession" to "dismissal" and "consolation". All of this, as I remembered more and more clearly, was to be seen in Varga's remarkable work.

"Son of the Right Hand" was the name I privately gave to the great Swede (the expression is used for the chosen of the Lord, who is "Man"), but for the poem I chose a title and epigraph more appropriate to the silent, restrained sacrificial attitude of Wallenberg.

Let me note finally that the words "Khaya" and "Aum" are taken from the refrains of Hebrew lullabies.

January 1991

Donec eris felix, multos numerabis amicos:
tempora si tuerint nubila, solus eris.

(Когда хорошая погода – у тебя много друзей:
когда собираются тучи – ты одинок.)

Надпись на постаменте памятника
Валленбергу в Будапеште

1

это
нет никого… – на поверку: давно завершившийся
общий
единый
последний отъезд –

как остановленный мир –

(и осталась – оставшемуся
долгая
смятая влажность
– где-то на шее на лацканах на рукавах –
долгого
старения множества глаз) –

это
дрожью застывший (как призрак ничтожный
вечности некой)
рот чернозубый
простого терновника –

от одинокой – все той же – руки отдаляющийся:

на расстоянии том же –

(рядом
здесь
в переулке) –

это город боярышников – август
Восемьдесят Восьмого – и ясным его средоточием
единственная всечеловеческая

Donec eris felix, multos numerabis amicos:
tempora si tuerint nubila, solus eris.

(When the weather is fine you have many friends:
when the clouds gather you are alone.)

Inscription on the monument to Raoul
Wallenberg in Budapest

1

this
is *no-one here...* – but in fact: the long since completed
common
and single
final departure –

like a world stopped short –

(and there remained – to the one remaining
the long
crumpled dampness
– somewhere on the neck on lapels on sleeves –
of the long
growing old of a host of eyes) –

this
is the frozen-in-trembling (insubstantial spectre
of some eternity)
black-toothed mouth
of the simple thorn –

keeping far from the lonely – unchanging – hand:

at the very same distance –

(here
nearby
in the alley) –

this town of hawthorns – August
Eighty-Eight – and in its clear centre
this single all-human

рука – это очень давно
простая уже Простота
вечности-нищенски-простенькой: как
истоптанные туфельки
в Стро-е-ниях Вечных
для
Печей и Волос… –

2

город шиповников… – не отдыхает
лишь эта
рука: воплотилась
в Утешение вечное
давно утешенных: осталась – о : без
кого и чего – Утешающая
самая
одинокая в мире
рука –

"вот" – остановилась – "вот
дверь"
(больше сказать – означало бы
сдвинуть
Бога того же: чтоб
более – быть
влажной-костлявостью-хрупкостью
в большей Покинутости): "вот
(просто вагонная)
дверь" – и *отнятие*
медленно-вечное
простое – руки:

Мир
Без Никого –

:

(только дрожание слабое:

Х а - а й - й я…) –

hand – this from long ago
is just plain Simplicity
of beggarly-plain-eternity: like
down-at-heel slippers
in those Eternal Con-struc-tions
for
Gas Chambers and Hair… –

2

town of wild roses – only this hand
never rests:
it is incarnate
in eternal Consolation
of the long-since consoled: it remains – oh: with
no-one and nothing – the Consoling
the most
lonely hand
in the world –

"here" – it has stopped – "here
is the door"
(to say more – would be
to displace
that same God: and thus
still more – to be
damp-boniness-fragility
in greater Abandonment): "here
is the (railway-truck)
door" – and the *simple*
slowly-eternal
removal – of the hand:

World
With No-one –

:

(only a faint trembling

Kha – ay – ya…) –

3

давно
с Небом Бессловесия давно попрощавшись
нескончаемо опускается в ров
страшную бла-гос-лов-ляет
Землю – к а к   К л а д о в у ю (о сколько об этом
знаю
будто Вселенною-Сном) –

влажная
от пара незримого крови –

(рядом – приподымаются
в поте
холмы – шевелящиеся
из дальних долин и клочками-тряпья-только-
                                          ветру-молившиеся
спины... – давно не шелохнутся
молчат как рука – и уже никогда
не дрогнет
рука) –

– ушли поезда:

о: *Х а й - й я ...* –

А - а - у м ... –

и Время
призрачноепадальное – стало
минутою
(о наконец) провожания
давно –

Давно-Бесконечной... –

:

(... п о ю т ...) –

3

long ago
parting long ago with the *Heaven of Wordlessness*
it unendingly sinks to the pit
in be-ne-dic-tion of the terrible
Earth – *like a Store-House* (oh how much of this
I know
as through Universe-Sleep) –

damp
with the steam of unseen blood –

(nearby they lift themselves
in sweat
the hills – stirring
out of distant valleys – and with-tattered-rags-to-the-
                                        wind-only-praying
the backs ... long since unmoving
silent as the hand – and now never
again will it tremble
the hand) –

– the trains have departed:

oh: *Khay-ya...* –

A-a-um... –

and Time
carrion-spectral – has become
the minute
(oh at last) of farewell
long ago –

Long-Ago-and-Endless... –

:

(...*they sing*...) –

4

это
Единственный Уровень:
Выше – разбрелись говоря-допевая
Ниже
Договаривают Руке (и кричат) – вот такая
Троица
в зное палящем –

(ибо
Посредине – Рука) –

в городе боярышников (всегда разверзались
в тех
переулках-и-криках
о
черными ртами) –

и – снова
вторгается жалкое
детское *пляско-подобие*
без никого:

X а - а й - й я –

(нет даже призрака воздуха) –

о: *А у м* ... –

5

– вдруг ударяет в лицо : а была же
другая рука
белая – на красных перилах балкона
рядом с азалиями –

(вздрогнула вдруг и исчезла
и мир
стал – сверлящею точкой во лбу:

о: это
первое *средоточие страха*... –

– *а ведь не было крикнуто "мама"*) ... –

4

this
is the One Level
Higher – they have scattered speaking-and-singing
Lower
They Keep Speaking to the Hand (and shouting) – such is
the Trinity
in the blazing heat –

(for
In the Middle is the Hand) –

in the town of hawthorns (always gaping
in those
alleys-and-shouts
oh
black-mouthed) –

and – again
comes in the pitiful
childish *dance-likeness*
with no-one:

Kha-ay-ya –

(not even a ghost of air) –

oh: *Aum...* –

5

– a sudden blow to the face: for there was
another hand
white – on red balcony railings
beside the azaleas –

(suddenly it shuddered and vanished
and the world
became – a piercing nail in the forehead:

oh: this
first *centre of fear...* –

– *and yet no-one there shouted out* "mother")... –

6

миром
стало молчанье руки – и продрогшая треснувшая
н е   о с т а в л я я
давно отпустила (такая
прощается – *лишь для себя*
никогда не прощаясь):

как остановившийся Бог
(больше
иного не будет – иного
кроме
Его Остановки) –

вот
это м е с т о
руки ... – и над нею
Гу-бы Гля-дя-щие:

так – словно в легком полете
смотрят чуть вздрагивая
лишь – на детей... –

(и
как смешалась
потом
с этой навязчивой детскостью
смя-та-я немощь све-че-ни-я
бедненько-свято-вокруг-становящихся
кем-то оплаканных
тел – ведь действительно: как *матерьялов*
да только
в с е   ж е – Господних...) –

7

и приснившееся Времяподобие
восходящее (Куда-Восходящее)
давно – без движения: стало последней
бескрайне-единой
минутой Спасания (*лязг:*

6

the silence of the hand
became a world – and soaked through cracked open
still not abandoning
it had long since dismissed (such a hand
takes leave – *for itself alone*
never taking leave):

like God stopped short
(no other
will there be – no other
only
His Stopping) –

here
in this *place*
of the hand... – and above it
the Gaze of the Lips:

so – as if in light flight
barely trembling you look
only – at children... –

(and
how afterwards
mingled
with this childlike importunity
the crushed in-fir-mi-ty of ra-di-ance
of holy-beggarly-bystanding
lamented by somebody
bodies – yes indeed: as of *materials*
but still
even so – the Lord's...) –

7

and the dreamed-of Timelikeness
ascending (Whither-Ascending)
long since – without movement: became
the last boundlessly-single
moment of Rescue (the *clang:*

... будто – весь в пальцах... – с иглою
Господи! – шубертовской... – *лязг*):

лицо переходит
темнея
в продолжение
Двери Последней:

(о сколько же было: *поля* и *долины*
сплошь
из *черных*
дверей)... –

:

о: *Х а й я* ... –

8

быть может
я – Сон без Себя
где пели смеялись и плакали
сразу же стали нигде а поют
только рука не прощается
с Уровнем
своим над Землею: ушли и уйдут
и только она остается: сквозь ветки
глядят
облака
(о – грязнозубые) –

– ушли поезда – лишь гармоника
одна на всю Землю
поет
в мире
рваным кустом продолжая боярышниковым
дождь и свое одиночество:

Х а - а й - й я...

Август 1988, Будапешт

... as if – piercing his finger... – with the needle
oh God! – Schubert's needle... – the *clang*):

the face darkening
becomes
a continuation
of the Final Door:

(oh how many there were: *fields* and *valleys*
all
from the *black*
doors)... –

:

oh: *Khaya*... –

8

maybe
I am Dream without Self
where they sang laughed and wept
straight away they were nowhere but they sing
only the hand does not leave
its Level
above Earth: they went and will go
and it only remains: through branches
stare
clouds
(oh – dirty-toothed) –

– the trains have departed – the harmonica
alone to the whole Earth
sings
in the world
in a tattered hawthorn bush continuing
the rain and its solitude:

Kha-ay-ya...

August 1988, Budapest

ПОКЛОН – ПЕНИЮ

(Тридцать шесть вариаций на темы чувашских
и татарских народных песен)

2

Был конь у меня, –
хоть растянись ты на нем и поспи!
На крупе могла, не расплескиваясь,
держаться вода.

10

Стан мой легкий, глаза мои черные
в этом огне хоровода родного
горят, быть может,
в последний раз.

11

Не уменьшить мне боль,
полдуши в этом поле оставив!
Молчу я, и лишь за холмом, как ребенок,
громко плачет куница.

12

Прибыли мы за невестою
с сердцем белым,
сделаем свадьбу
белее снега.

13

Если запустить мое пенье
ладом скользящим,
лучшая песенка выкатится
клубком золотым.

20

Все настойчивей зов одинокий
иволги – за околицей,
подружки невесты задвигались,
как овсяные снопы золотые.

SALUTE – TO SINGING

(Thirty-six variations on themes from Chuvash and Tatar folksongs)

2

Once I had a horse, –
you could stretch out on him and sleep!
Water could lie on his back
and not a drop spill.

10

My slender figure, my dark eyes
burn in the fire
of our native dance
for the last time, perhaps.

11

There's no way to still my pain,
half my soul remains in that field!
I say nothing, but beyond the hill like a child
a marten weeps out loud.

12

We have come for the bride
with the snow-white heart,
let us make a wedding
brighter than snow.

13

If I set my singing
on a slippery track,
the best song will roll out
like a golden ball.

20

Ever stronger the lonely call
of the oriole – outside the village,
the bridesmaids have set forth
like sheaves of golden oats.

23

Отправилась милая в путь, и черная ласточка
навстречу ночи
мчится – по крыльям лия
ручьи дождевые.

24

А богата была – девятью походками:
чередовались-играли!
Потом
жизнь оставила – только одну.

26

Встречая меня,
отец мой раскатывается, как шелковый тюк,
скатывается обратно,
меня проводив.

29

Точно конопляное поле отцовское,
ровны лесные вершины,
плывет моя песня над ними,
будто поет это – лес.

30

В поле – зеленого жаль,
жаль – золотого над полем!
Брат мой, стареем,
седеем, как синие бусы.

31

Принесли мы изящество ног,
чтобы
в памяти вашей оставить!
Разрешите нам пляску последнюю.

23

The beloved set out, and a black swallow
flies to meet
the night – pouring from her wings
the streaming rain.

24

And she was rich – with nine ways of walking:
one-after-another in play!
Then life
left her with just the one.

26

Coming out to meet me,
my father rolls out like a skein of silk,
and then rolls up again,
having seen me off.

29

Like our father's field of hemp,
the forest tops are level,
over them swims my song
as if the forests were singing.

30

In the field – pity for the green!
Pity for the gold overhead!
Brother, we are growing old,
growing grey like blue beads.

31

We have brought the beauty of legs,
so that in your memory
it will remain!
Allow us this one last dance.

35

Хватит, покружились мы здесь,
как звонкие монеты серебряные,
поклонимся – согнемся пред вами,
как белые деньги бумажные.

36

И там, где стояли мы,
пусть останется
свечение – нашего
благословения.

1988–91

35

Enough, we have swung and swung
like ringing silver coins,
we shall bow, shall bend before you
like paper money, all white.

36

And where we stood,
may there remain
the shining of our
benediction.

1988–91

ВСЕ ДАЛЬШЕ В СНЕГА

После гибели Т. Х.
(или – "Памяти ангела")

Бываешь – Прям?
ну что же –

опять я – зная всю никчемность
упоминаю Силу – словом:

– все ту же нечтость Глыбы-Анонима
верней – Аморфности-да-Анонима-тьму! –

(итак – подбрасываются нам – к р у ш е н ь я!.. –

движенье-аноним: руками смертных
столь мощно Рушит – "не мытьем так катаньем":

поверишь – Не-при-я-ти-ем!..) –

Содержится ль – как "что-то" – в прахе?
мы – средь останков: "как-то" там
не просто… не одни останки… –

(быть может – и движений нет…) –

. . . . –

пора – на пробу:
выпадом
разрывом! –

я – заскорузл – из давней глуби нов
забытой мною прямотой:

– я сплю – давно *духовным сном*
а снег
работает в полях – в ложбинах – как крестьянин
(скромней поэта истинный поэт)
и просыпаюсь – воплощеньем
какой-то новой тишины – без просьб
держащейся как в прахе воздух –

EVER FURTHER INTO THE SNOWS

After the death of T. Kh.
(or – "To the memory of an angel")

are You sometimes – Upright?
what then –

once again I – knowing its pointlessness
mention – with a word – the Power:

– unchanging somethingness of Clod-Anonymity
or rather – dark-of-Amorphous-Anonymity! –

(and so – they fling us – *catastrophes!* ... –

movement-anonymous: with hands of mortals
so mightily Destroys – "by hook or by crook":

you'll believe – by Non-ac-qui-es-cence! ...) –

is it – like "something" – Contained in dust?
we are among remnants: "somehow" there
is not simple... not remnants alone... –

(perhaps – there is not even movement...) –

. . . . –

it is time – for the test:
by assault
by rupture! –

I – calloused – am renewed from old depths
by uprightness long forgotten:

– I sleep – a long-ago *sleep of the spirit*
but snow
works in the fields – in the gulleys – like a peasant
(true poet more modest than a poet)
and I wake – the incarnation
of some new quietness – without questions
hanging like air in the dust –

когда уже не страшны и возмездья
которыми лже-небеса бесцентровые
свисают в снах из бедных сил!.. –

не говорю "я так живу" – движенье-жизнь моя
                                                    слабей желаний-ходьб:

– и где-то только суета Пост-Фактум
перетворцов – все тех же переделателей
все той же Призрака-Страны –

а пустота – такая вот огромность
моя – пустая: Право Равнодушия –

(не людям ложь! – самоотмена слова) –

и все же – завершеньем – вею:

я – осыпаюсь: будто в мире су-ще-ству-ю-щем
все ту же нечтость тьмы-и-анонима
"господней" – *по привычке* – именуя
в видениях без боли сотрясаю
отвалами моими и паденьями:

как черноту безвидности-безмира! –

а бездна никакая – а удары
из ни-ка-кой-то-сти! и с чем – разрыв? –

когда во всем – безместно – но во всем
лишь безымянность и отсутствие –

и для того – чтоб более я был?.. –

теперь уже и этого не нужно:

(а что Е м у - Ч е м у – да впрочем что и мне…) –

и меньшим дрогну я – чтоб завершиться большим:

пора – самоотменою оставить
то что казалось (или было) лучшим –

when even reprisals are no longer terrible
in which pseudo-heavens uncentred
hang in dreams made of beggarly powers!... –

I do not say "I live so" – my life-movement is weaker than
                                                    wish-walking:

– and somewhere is only the vain fuss Post-Factum
of the recreators – still the same remakers
of the same Spectre-Country –

but the emptiness – such vastness
of mine – all empty: Right of Indifference –

(no lie for people! self-cancelling word) –

and still – in conclusion – I am blown:

I crumble: as if in the world ex-ist-ing
still naming – *out of habit* – as "the lord's"
that same somethingness of dark-anonymity
in visions without pain I convulse
with my tumbles with my falls:

the blackness it seems of unvision-unworld! –

but no abyss is there – but the blows
from non-being-ness! and with what – the rupture? –

when in everything – placeless – but in everything
there is only namelessness absence –

and in order – that I should be more?...–

now even this is not needed:

(and what is it to *Some-Him* – and what is it to me...) –

and I shudder in the lesser – to conclude in the greater:

it is time – by self-cancelling to leave
what seemed (or was) the best –

(да будет это – проблеском последним):

Что-Светло-Даже-То-Что-Мне-Уже-Не-Веровать! –

(уйдя – давно уже – в снега)

1986–87

(and let this be – a final glimmer):

What-Is-Light-Even-That-I-Can-No-Longer-Believe! –

(going out – for a long time now – into the snows)

1986–87

СТРАНА-ПРОЛОГ

чистота тропинки
простота воды –

и такое небо – будто снится
этой выси – никому неведомая
очень – даже очень уж – другая
бедность ясная Земли –

в нас немного говорящей:

"пока мы в мире есть
дым – в трубах изб – играет"

1994

САД – ГРУСТЬ

это
(быть может)
ветер
клонит – такое легкое
(для смерти)
сердце

1994

COUNTRY-PROLOGUE

cleanness of the path
simplicity of water –

and such a sky – as if a dream
of this height – unknown to all
very – oh yes very – different
bright poverty of Earth –

speaking a little in us:

"while we are in the world
smoke – in cottage chimneys – plays"

1994

GARDEN – GRIEF

this
(maybe)
is the wind
bending – so light
(for death)
a heart

1994

ЭПИЛОГ С ПОЛЕМ

что-то тускло-белое больничное
в поле двигало скольжения
– дай нам Бог лечиться этой тишиной –
и дорога за окном как за воротами
угасала все сырее и грустнее
"вот и весь" шепталось будто "путь земной"

1994

EPILOGUE WITH FIELD

something hospital-dimly-white
in the field slid and shifted
– God grant us this quietness cure us –
and the road out of the window as if beyond gates
was fading ever damper and more sadly
"there" as if whispered "is all our earthly road"

1994

Notes

Beginning (1954). The Russian version of this poem was translated literally from the original Chuvash, and was included by the author in his collections to characterize the stage in his work when he was moving from writing in Chuvash to writing in Russian.

Presentiment of a requiem (1957). After its composition this poem became connected with the figure of Boris Pasternak.

Death (1960). Aygi's mother died in his native village of Shaymurzino in 1960.

Morning in childhood (1961). The vowel "a" has particular importance for Aygi, being associated with origins and with pristine purity.

Bird from beyond the seas (1962). The bird from beyond the seas is a creature from Russian folk legend. The dedicatee of this poem, the composer Andrey Volkonsky, was a leading member of the artistic circle to which Aygi belonged in the 1960s.

Kazimir Malevich (1962). The painter Malevich has been a major source of inspiration for Aygi (see Introduction, p. 23). The "boards" referred to here are the wooden base for icon-painting. Vitebsk, Chagall's native town, was the site of the UNOVIS art school where Malevich and El Lissitsky worked. "Velimir" is the Futurist poet Velimir Khlebnikov. Daniil Kharms was a leading avant-garde poet of the 1920s. Before his death Malevich made a Suprematist sketch for his own coffin.

Morning in August (1963). For a discussion of this poem see P. France, *Poets of Modern Russia*, pp. 210-12.

For Dedication of childhood: cleaning walnuts (1964). This title, like many of Aygi's, links this poem to previous ones; *Degree: of Stability* includes both a poem entitled "Dedicated to childhood" and another entitled "For Dedication of childhood").

Dawn: in the intervals of sleep (1965). The phrase "néant de voix" comes from Kafka's story "The Singer Josefine, or the Mouse People", which Aygi read in French. He has continued to revere Kafka's memory (see "For a conversation about K.", 1967).

CONSOLATION: 3/24 (1965–67). The title of this book refers to the three hours of the day when poetic work was possible at this time.

House of the poet in Vologda (1966). The Russian poet Konstantin Batyushkov

(1787–1855), who influenced Pushkin, succumbed to mental illness and spent the last 30 years of his life in the northern town of Vologda. Prince Vyazemsky (1792–1878) was a poet, a friend of Batyushkov, and a prominent literary figure in early nineteenth-century Russia.

Roses in August (1966). For a discussion of this poem see Appendix.

For a conversation about K. – to Olga Mashkova (1967). K. is of course Kafka.

Consolation: field (1967). Aygi has written that in the Chuvash pagan religion the field was "the prototype of spiritual freedom".

Field near Ferapontovo (1967). Ferapontovo is the site of a celebrated monastery in northern Russia.

ČERNÁ HODINKA (1970–73). The title of this book is a Czech phrase meaning "a little dark hour", i.e. a twilight conversation.

Field: in the full blaze of winter (1970). Aygi has written of the dedicatee, René Char, in a note "Sur la mort de René Char" in G. Aïgui, *Conversations à distance*, tr. L. Robel (Saulxures, France, 1995), pp. 195-98.

At night: shuddering (1971). This poem is dedicated to the memory of Anatoly Mittov (1932–71), probably the most important artist of modern Chuvashia (for examples of his work see the article by Troels Andersen in the Danish periodical *CRAS*, 31 (1982), pp. 24-33).

Field: mist (1971). Aygi's sister Eva Lisin is a children's writer. The poem contains references to the death of their mother (see "Death", 1960).

QUIETNESS-PREMONITION (1974–76). On this book see Introduction, pp. 23–24.

Forest places: variation (1974). Psychiatric hospitals were used in Russia in the Brezhnev years to imprison and harass political dissidents.

Note: Apophatic (1976). The word "Apophatic" is in English in the original. It is a theological term referring to the knowledge of God gained through negation.

Willow branch at the window (1976). On this poem and the death of Konstantin Bogatyryov, translator of Rilke, see Introduction, pp. 23–24. The following three poems also refer to Bogatyryov's death. A "zek" is a (political) prisoner. "Their papers" and similar phrases refer to the KGB.

TIME OF GRATITUDE (1976–77). This radiant book carries the epigraph: "Night is the best time for believing in the light" (attributed to Plato). It was composed in the summer months of 1976 and 1977 in a country region near Leningrad.

House outside town (1977). The images here refer back to "Willow branch at the window" in the previous book.

You-Day (1977). See Appendix for a discussion of this poem.

Dream: friends and you (1979). The epigraph is from a poem by Pasternak.

VERONICA'S BOOK (1983–84). On this book see Introduction, p. 26, and for a discussion of "Continuation of the 'period of likenesses' " see Appendix.
Little song for you – about your father (1983). This poem is based on a folksong included in *An Anthology of Chuvash Poetry*, p. 57.

Epilogue: Suvalkiya lullaby (1984). The words given in italic are Lithuanian.

The last Ravine (1983). Aygi has written a short text devoted to the German poet Paul Celan; Léon Robel's French translation, entitled "Au souffle", is published in *Le Nouveau Commerce*, 81 (1991). Ravines are an important feature of the Chuvash countryside, and were a place of refuge for the people in times of persecution.

Burning – during harvest (1983). On the translation of this poem see my essay in *Comparative Criticism*, 16 (1994).

Final departure (1988). Raoul Wallenberg, a diplomat in the Swedish embassy in Budapest during World War Two, was instrumental in saving thousands of Jews from the extermination camps. At the end of the war he was seized by Russian security forces and disappeared. Only in 1989 was it reported in Stockholm that according to Soviet sources he had been executed in a Soviet gaol in 1947, at the age of 35. Aygi's poem was given a full-page spread in *Literaturnaya Gazeta* in 1991.

Country-Prologue (1994). The last two lines (a literal translation from the Chuvash) are quoted in his notebooks by the great Chuvash poet Vasley Mitta (1908–57) as he remembered them from the singing of his father, the illiterate peasant Yagur Mitta.

Reading Aygi[1]

Aygi is often thought of as a hermetic poet, more difficult than he really is. In this essay I set out to describe some of the formal features of three of his poems and thus to reach a fuller understanding of them. This may mean doing a kind of violence to the poems, which should work in their own way, rustling and whispering rather than affirming or describing, but this kind of close attention seems essential when translating, and I hope it will be of interest to readers of my translations. I refer primarily to the Russian texts, but most of my remarks relate almost as much to the English translations.

"Roses in August" (*Consolation 3/24*, 1965–67)
"Rozy v Avguste" (*Utesheniye 3/24*)

The fraction in the title of the book from which this brief poem comes refers to the three hours out of twenty-four when poetry can be written. Four other poems in the book have roses in the title: "Consolation: roses" ("Utesheniye: rozy"); "And: the roses lose their petals" ("I: ottsvetayut rozy"); "And: after the roses" ("I: posle roz"); "Roses from the end" ("Rozy s kontsa"). The roses are always white and they are fragile. Another recurrent element in this book is the reference to physical violence; three titles contain the phrase *vosklitsaniye byushchikh* ("exclamation of beaters"). Titles are very important; often, as here, they are the one element in the poem that attaches it clearly to some object in the physical world, thus directing the reader's interpretation. The epigraph too adds something; the quotation from Annensky brings two further physical items (willows, sand) into a poem that tends to abstraction, and the very name of the poet Innokenty Annensky (1856–1909) would suggest to Russian poetry-readers a combination of fragile beauty and nervous melancholy.

A striking formal feature of the Russian poem is its rhythmical structure – less apparent in the translation. The basic metre, which is not so noticeable on silent reading, is iambic; if one disregards the line endings, one sees that most of the poem can be read as quite regular four-foot iambics, mostly with masculine endings (lines 2, 5, 7, 13), but with feminine endings to lines 9 and 11 and a dactylic ending to line 8. The odd one out is line 3, also iambic, but a pentameter with dactylic ending. This ending, however, sets up a near-rhyme with line 8 (in both cases verbal adjectives signifying decay: "smouldering", "dying"). If one adds to this some import-ant sound repetitions (especially the *k-k-b-b* pattern at the begin-ning and centre), the overall effect is to bind the lines into a perceptible unity. The poem can be read as a single sentence.

Against this must be set the visual impact. Typography is used to suggest gaps, silences, white spaces in the poem, suspending the forward motion, allowing room for the unspoken thought. Punctuation reinforces this. Aygi rarely uses the capital letters and full stops of normal written discourse, or the commas that articu-late written language to suggest the rhythms of speech or the flow of ordered thought. Instead he uses signs in an original, deliberate way to break up his text and to suggest unexplored relationships between words and concepts; G. Janecek, in an article on Aygi's punctuation, writes of the use of the colon in one particular poem (not included here): "Throughout, these colons suggest a more intense relationship than mere insertion: if not always an obvious causality, then something close to it, and a constant shift of levels. Thus the colon serves to heighten metaphoric intensity to an unprecedented degree."[2] In "Roses in August" there are only three kinds of punctuation mark: exclamation mark, colon and dash – the last of these serves (among other things) to disrupt the iambic rhythm of lines 1-2 and 4-5. Fragmentation is opposed to unity.

Moving to syntax, one sees that the poem has no main verb, although the verb "to be" is understood in the opening exclama-tion – "oh [...] how [...] close [you are] to us". The whole poem seems to be a development of this apostrophe to roses (the "you" of lines 3 and 7), through the comparisons of the second, third and fourth "stanzas". There is some uncertainty about the links between the different lines, however. Line 5 may be read as belonging with line 4 (in which case the dash is a pause) or as a separate exclamation, set off by the two dashes on either side of it. Similarly, it is not clear whether the last stanza depends on the "when" of line 8 (as seems most probable) or whether it could not also be a new departure, following on from the first or second stanza. The reader has to hesitate, balanced between a unified and a discontinuous reading.

It is interesting to look at the use of different parts of speech, for here too there is a blurring of boundaries. There are few concrete nouns in the poem, and most of these are in the title or the epigraph – thereafter there is only *kost'* (bone) and – somewhat less concretely – *litso* (face). *Granitsy* (limits), *chuvstva* (feelings) and *bezdna* (abyss, pit) are all more abstract, or at any rate less precise. Then there are nouns derived from verbs – *proval* (collapse) and *lyubimaya* (loved one) – or from adjectives – *blizost'* (closeness), *drobnost'* (fracturation), *belizna* (whiteness). The parts of speech run together; there is an adjective (*umirayushchaya*, dying) and an adverb (*bolyashche*, painfully) derived from verbs and a participle (*razrushaya*, destroying) which hesitates between verb and adverb. This is not a clear-cut flower painting, but more like a vision between sleep and waking – as is confirmed by the words *slepya* (literally "blinding") and *mereshchitsya* (literally "appears like a mirage", here "we glimpse"). Moreover, the ambiguities I have mentioned in the syntax are echoed in the vocabulary, as the translator notes with regret. *Proval* suggests a gap or failure as well as "collapse", *tlet'* embodies a notion of warmth ("smoulder") but also decay, and *syroy* is both "damp" and raw.

What happens, then, is that the familiar image of roses offered by the title is dissolved in a swirl of qualities, processes and movements. These are then woven, by the reader, into a pattern of echoes and similitudes; in "Here" from *Beginnings of the Clearings* ("Zdes'", *Nachala polyan*, 1954–59) Aygi writes in Baudelairean fashion that "all things answer one another". In "Roses in August" the repeated *kak* (as) highlights this notion of correspondence. In the first place the "you" (roses) and the "we" of lines 3, 7 and 9 are brought into close proximity (lines 3 and 7) and seem to merge. The "face" or "faces" of lines 5 and 10 refer primarily to human faces, but the stress on their whiteness (in the final word, but also in the image of bone) brings them close to the white faces of the roses – which have of course been apostrophized at the outset.

There are two main thematic clusters in this poem, both already implicitly present in the title. The first concerns decline, collapse and death. The "August" of the title and the "late summer" of the epigraph both suggest a time of fragile beauty, the time when the roses are beginning to fade (see also "And: the roses lose their petals"). The third line expresses this decline in words that suggest the dying embers of a fire. Then, in the final section, the participle *razrushaya* (destroying) and the strange noun *drobnost'* (fracturation) drive home the image of disintegration. Beyond the falling white petals of the roses is the *bezdna* (abyss, pit), and this is clearly connected to the death of human beings in the third stanza and in the word *kost'* (bone) in the second stanza (the skull beneath the skin).

The image of bone is a bridge to the second thematic group, that of whiteness. Quantitatively, this is less in evidence than disintegration, but if we understand the roses of the title to be white (as I think we must, having reflected on the whole poem), then images of white are placed at the very beginning and end, containing and transcending the collapse. The word *slepya* (blinding) also suggests to me the elimination of all colour in a whiteness like that of the snowstorm. A reading of Aygi's work as a whole reveals the extreme importance of this notion; the whiteness of snow, bone and flowers (rose, jasmine, phlox, hawthorn) is seen in highly positive terms, an absolute of purity as in the paintings of Malevich (one of the poet's constant points of reference). White is connected with pain (*bolyashche*), and one should remember that this poem figures in a book full of physical violence – but it is a pain that is overcome in a hardly expressible, mystical vision of both death and being.

What I have just written is perhaps too explicit, since the essence of the poem lies precisely in the interplay between fragmentation and wholeness. The formal features indicate how the reader can be disoriented by the spacing, the uncertain syntax, the lexical ambiguities, the blurring of concrete and abstract, human and non-human. If nevertheless the overriding impression left by the poem is positive and unified, this is partly because of the placing of the images of whiteness, but above all, I think, because of the rhythmical organization of the whole. The iambic metre strides over such irregularities as those of line 3, and the final four lines, while they incorporate destruction, do so with a rhythm that is both traditional and affirmative.

"You-Day" (*Time of Gratitude*, 1976–77)
"Ty-Den'" (*Pora blagodarnosti*)

I think one can detect in this poem too, written some eleven years later in 1977, something of the same tension between opposites. Here the title gives less away. The capital letter on "Day" indicates a certain solemnity, but who is "you" (more literally, "thou")? It helps to read the poem in the context of the book in which it appears: *Time of Gratitude* (*Pora blagodarnosti*) consists of poems written in the aftermath of the violent death of the poet's friend, the poet and translator Konstantin Bogatyryov (see Introduction, p. 23). The book carries an epigraph attributed to Plato: "The night is the best time for believing in the light." Death and resurrection are central themes. It may be over-simple to read the "you" of the title and of lines 3, 4, and 14 as an apostrophe to the dead friend, but this is at any rate a start for a reading.

Again the metre is iambic, and this is underlined by the "poetic" spellings of *vetr* (wind) and *mertsaniye* (shimmering) in lines 2 and 4. Lines 4-7 half-conceal in their arrangement on the page a quite regularly stressed and eloquent pair of iambic pentameters. As in "Roses in August," the rhythmical impetus (like the flight of swifts?) binds the lines into a single movement. But here too continuity is balanced by fragmentation. The spacing is more noticeable (it is interesting that in the errata to the Syntaxis edition of his poems the author indicates the need for a space between lines 12 and 13). Dashes, colons, brackets and points all suspend the forward movement, suggesting snatches of thought, whispers, fragments... This can be seen if one follows the poem through from beginning to end.

As is often the case with Aygi, the opening "and" creates the impression that this is just a moment in an ongoing meditation. The beginning of the poem, however, reads at first like confident metrical discourse, written in the past tense and the third person. This is soon interrupted by the line-spacing, and even more so by brackets, which shift the poem to a different mode – after statement, exclamatory apostrophe; after the third person, the second person singular. The next four lines return to the more eloquent mode, emphasized by the metre and the exclamation mark. This could be seen to continue in lines 8 and 9, except that the punctuation of line 8 invites us to break the flow (like the spasmodic cries of swifts perhaps) and that the brackets suggest an aside, more hushed it seems, and referring to an image of tender fragility which occurs in a number of poems of this period relating to the death of Bogatyryov. From here to the end of the poem, although the metre remains the same, the impression of fragmentation increases, with not only brackets, dashes and spacing, but the suspension points of the penultimate line. It is as if the eloquence of the earlier lines fades out finally into almost inaudible whispering.

A striking and typical feature of "You-Day" is the creation of com-

pound words. The poet seems to compensate for the dislocation of
the syntax by forging words together into a new unity. This begins in
the title, continues in *mertsaniyem-molitvoy* (shimmering-and-prayer)
and *ditya-dusha* (child-soul) and culminates in *naskvoz'-nedosyagaye-
most'* (through-and-through-inaccessibility). The last of these com-
binations, given prominence by occupying an entire line, reads like
an oxymoron, bringing together suggestions of penetration and
impenetrability. As I see it, this highlights a contrast that is central to
the poem. On the one hand there is the separation of swifts from
observer, poet from world, dead from living. But against this,
through these compound words and in other ways, there is the
notion of connectedness. The wind (bearing happiness) reaches to
the heart of the swifts, "you" is in everything, the "Day" prays for
"you", against the inaccessibility of the swifts' cry stands the notion
of openness, the beam of light of line 11 envelops everything, and
the word *slukh* (hearing) at the end of the poem brings together the
poet, the birds and the absent (yet present) "you". As the *proshchaya*
(forgiving) of line 5 suggests, this is a poem of reconciliation.

It would be possible to go much further in interpreting "You-
Day". One could explore the connotations of the swift, and the
intertextual echoes between this poem and poems about swifts by
(for instance) Pasternak and René Char. Is the swift the bird of
poetry, the bird of imagination? If the poem is indeed to be read in
relation to the death (one year earlier) of Kostya Bogatyryov, then
should one not see in the image of the swift and in the closing reference to keen hearing a homage to a gifted poetic translator? I do
not think, however, that this kind of precise interpretation is neces-
sary or helpful, since the large images of the poem – day, wind,
light, cries – and the abstract notions and emotional impulses it
embodies can be related to many different personal experiences.

"Continuation of the 'period of likenesses'" (*Veronica's
Book*, 1983–84)
"Prodolzheniye 'perioda skhodstv'" (*Tetrad' Veroniki*)

The two poems considered so far both gain from being read in
the context of the books from which they are taken, even if such
contextualizing is not obligatory. For the third poem, the context
would seem essential. Its very title indicates that this is one of a
series. More than this, it comes from a book more obviously unified than any of Aygi's earlier books, *Veronica's Book* (*Tetrad' Vero-*

niki), which is made up of poems written over a period of a few months in 1983, after the birth of the poet's daughter. As he notes in an afterword, these poems are the fruit of hours of close contact between father and baby; many of them, including this one, are notations of particular moments.

This time, there is no difficulty in identifying the subject: the poet, watching his daughter's changing face, sees hints of likenesses which connect the baby with the life of his family and of the whole Chuvash people. Impelled by a supple ternary metre, the poem moves steadily forward (with no line spacing), even if this motion is all the time being slowed down by the familiar pauses of colon, dash and suspension points – and above all by question marks, for the whole poem is a series of questions, guesses, approximations. It is noticeable that the majority of the pauses do not correspond to line endings; more often than not the sense runs over from one line to the next. The rhythm of the poem thus corresponds to a continuing, if hesitant, quest. What is particularly worth analysing is the sequence of metaphors which express this.

The two previous poems both began from objects in the natural world (flowers, birds) and proceeded by abstraction to suggest parallels between these objects and human experience. Here the process seems to be reversed. The starting point is the child's face, which is connected in a series of tentative metaphors to natural forms, forces and objects – and thus to the country and people of origin. The first group, always essential for Aygi, is that of light and shade. The opening verb, all the more noticeable in Russian for being an unusual – though readily understood – formation (*promel'kivat'*, to flit by), immediately suggests a succession of visual impressions, like clouds crossing a landscape. *Ten'* (shade, shadow) is the first noun; in addition to its visual value, it evokes the "shades" of the dead, soon to be resurrected. Shadow is followed by light in line 4, and again the participle *vspykhnuvshey* (flashing) of line 6, directly followed by the contrasting verbs *belet'* (to be white) and *temnet'* (to be dark). The light gleams fleetingly in line 8, then shines out triumphantly in line 12, where it is the light of the whole people, reflected in the sleeping face.

A second group of metaphors, equally important, is that of concealment and revelation. The child's *oblik* (appearance) has to be brought out of the distant past, hence the repeated images of depth, the notion of treasure buried in silent oblivion (line 3), the related verbs of uncovering (line 4) and raising up (line 6), the idea of a person lost and searching in a "first circle" (lines 9-11), and the concealed features of line 14. Two other metaphors are worthy of comment, in that they introduce a note of energy or even violence into this poem about a baby. The first is that of the storm (line 11); this connects with the wind of line 7, both being related to the past of the Chuvash people and their ancient "field" (a central image for Aygi, suggesting the spiritual freedom of traditional Chuvash society). The storm is a life-giving wind. And the second metaphor also invokes a time-honoured notion, that of forging or hammering out (line 13); as in "Roses in August", pain is associated here with illumination.

I have tried in these few pages to describe the original way Aygi uses words in poetry and also, though less fully, to suggest partial interpretations of three poems. It will be seen that some of the initial difficulties experienced by the reader are removed or attenuated by a greater awareness of their poetic context. I would not wish, however, to provide a *key* to the reading of Aygi, since his poems, like many poems of this century, should impel all readers to work out their own reading. In this the reader is in a similar position to the translator, except that the latter is often obliged to ride roughshod over the ambiguities that the former can maintain in all their unresolved richness.

NOTES

1 Adapted from an article published in *Essays in Poetics*, 12,1 (1987).
2 G. Janecek, "The Poetics of Punctuation in Gennadyj Ajgi's Verse", *Slavic and East European Journal*, 40, 2 (1996).

Further Reading

WORKS IN RUSSIAN

Stikhi, 1954–71, Otto Sagner, Munich, 1975

Otmechennaya zima, Syntaxis, Paris, 1982

Tetrad' Veroniki, bilingual French-Russian, Le Nouveau Commerce, tr. L. Robel, Paris, 1984

Vremya ovragov, bilingual French-Russian, Le Nouveau Commerce, tr. L. Robel, Paris, 1990

Zdes', Sovremennik, Moscow, 1991

Posledniy ot'ezd, Literaturnaya Gazeta, Moscow, 6 March 1991; bilingual German-Russian, Rainer Verlag, tr. F. P. Ingold, Berlin, 1993

Teper' vsegda snega, Sovetskiy Pisatel', Moscow, 1992

Poklon – peniyu, bilingual German-Russian, Rainer Verlag, tr. F. P. Ingold, Berlin, 1992

Tetrad' Veroniki, bilingual Polish-Russian, Świat literacki, Warsaw, 1995

Strana-Prolog, Izdaniye N. Dronnikova, Paris, 1995

Tetrad' Veroniki, Gileya, Moscow, 1997

ENGLISH TRANSLATIONS

Veronica's Book, Polygon, tr. P. France, Edinburgh, 1989

An Anthology of Chuvash Poetry, tr. P. France, Forest Books, London, 1991

Salute – to Singing, bilingual English-Russian, tr. P. France, Akros, Edinburgh, 1995

There are further translations by Edwin Morgan in *Cencrastus*, 1 (1979) and *Scottish Journal of Slavonic Studies*, 1 (1983); and by Peter France in *South-East Arts Review* (Summer 1978), *Comparative Criticism*, 4 (1982), *Cencrastus*, 16 (1984), *Verse*, 5, 1 (1988), *Chapman*, 55-56 (1989), *Temenos*, 10 (1989), *Lines Review*, 109 (1989) and *Tel Aviv Review*, 3 (1991)

CRITICISM

L. Robel, *Aïgui*, Seghers, Paris, 1993

P. France, *Poets of Modern Russia*, Cambridge University Press, 1982, pp. 210-19

P. France, "The Poetry of Gennady Aygi: a translator's reading", *Essays in Poetics*, 12, 1 (1987), pp. 1-14

P. France, "Translating a Chuvash poet: Gennady Aygi", *Comparative Criticism*, 16 (1994), pp. 187-94

G. Janecek, "The Poetics of Punctuation in Gennadyj Ajgi's Verse", *Slavic and East European Journal*, 40, 2 (1996)

INTERVIEWS

with James Vladimir Gill, *Frank*, 13 (1991), pp. 78-85
with Andrew Digby, *Verse*, 10, 2 (1993), pp. 81-85
with Irena Maryniak, *Index on Censorship*, 22, 10 (1993), pp. 29-30

Указатель Произведений

Index of Titles